Marketing at a Crossroads

A Look at the Major Challenges to Marketing and Transportation

Library of Congress Catalog Card No. 79-185558

published by
Public Relations Department
American Trucking Associations
Washington, D.C.
January, 1972

written by William F. Fuchs

Contents

1640964

Marketing
at a
Crossroads

Introduction

THIS VOLUME proceeded from a series of expository papers entitled, "Current Report, Motor Transport Economics."

The series, which examined in depth major trends and developments of the trucking industry and related areas of interest, quickly gained recognition among transportation executives, teachers, and others in the business community who found them to be authoritative, informative, and provocative.

American Trucking Associations functioned as publisher for the series, furnishing writers, editors, researchers, and consultants who worked on the various issues.

From the first issue, United States Steel has sponsored the publication and distribution of Current Report as a project of the ATA Foundation. Both United States Steel and the ATA Foundation embraced the series as a significant contribution to the marketing and transportation industry.

With the issuance of Number 27, published in May 1971, it was felt that the objectives of the Current Report series—to stimulate its readers and alert them to major changes and influences in transportation and related areas—had been met, and it was decided to conclude the project.

However, the final three issues—on "marketing" —have received such uncommon interest and praise that the sponsors and publisher have been stimulated to produce this hard-cover volume for distribution beyond those audiences served by Current Report's regular circulation.

Introduction

The subjects explored here involve tremendous change brought on by ecological, social, and technological forces, which are shaping and modifying today's world with unprecedented swiftness.

Ecological change, social change, technological change—these are the three dimensions of environment from which there is no escape. Man must respond to such challenges, and primary among his responses will be those he makes in the world of transportation and marketing.

Man has newly awakened to the very real threat of pollution—pollution of water and air and land. But it is not a problem that stands in isolation. It is inextricably linked with the social challenges of population growth, megalopolitan living, and growing affluence, while both the ecological and social forces are related to and affected by the unrelenting technological revolution that is exerting exciting changes in lifestyles with unbelievable speed.

These, then, are the great issues covered in this book, with emphasis on the role of transportation and marketing in this ever-changing world.

Speaking for the publisher and the sponsors, we express the hope that this provocative book will contribute to and stimulate the many marketing executives and students and all others among its readers who in the foreseeable future will pursue such change and challenges.

Walter F. Carey

Walter F. Carey, Chairman
The ATA Foundation

Foreword

THIS BOOK was written by William F. Fuchs of the American Trucking Associations staff. Among the many Government departments and agencies which were of invaluable help to the writer in his research were The White House, Congress, the Departments of Agriculture, Defense, Labor, and Transportation, the Interstate Commerce Commission, and the National Aeronautics and Space Administration. Private business, too, was a big contributor—from United States Steel, ITT, AT&T, and other major manufacturing corporations, to airlines and motor truck transportation companies. Newspapers, magazines, other periodicals, books, and TV scripts also were consulted freely. A number of ATA staff executives and experts from United States Steel contributed from their expertise. ATA's Department of Research & Transport Economics gave the manuscripts careful examination, as did staff members of the sponsor, United States Steel.

The help of each and every one is greatly appreciated.

1

Transportation
and
Ecology

Chapter One

Transportation
and
Ecology

The
Crossroads

From Daniel Boone to Neil Armstrong: In less than 200 years, American man has hacked his way through a Kentucky wilderness, spanned a continent, perfected his machines, conquered the skies, and set foot on the moon.

Now the stars themselves beckon. A look at the miracles of the recent past virtually removes all skepticism about the wondrous possibilities of the future.

America's dramatic growth, both physical and technological, has in a large sense been the story of growth in transportation. Man's ability to come up with various improvements in the art of transporting himself and his needs and wants has been the catalyst which has sent him spiraling forward and upward in a marvelous, ever-changing advancement. A magnificent system of transportation has made the American man the affluent man.

And that transportation system, in turn, owes the splendor of its achievement to the ever-improving technical skill that has produced steam locomotion, the internal combustion engine, the modern highway, and the airplane.

In other words, man's progress up from a primitive tribal existence and his ability to move himself and his goods from one geographic point to another are so intertwined that each is an integral part of the other. You might say that man's progress has journeyed along the same road man has carved to carry himself and his goods.

The marketing of goods is the very foundation of our civilization. Without it, all of the aesthetics that really make life worth while would crumble to dust. For man must eat before he can dream, and he must be able to feed, clothe, and shelter himself and his family before he can write, paint, philosophize, and, yes— even pray.

In his long, dramatic journey from tree and cave to tea and symphony, man

1

now has arrived at a major crossroads. Heretofore, while the road was often arduous and dangerous, it was always clearly marked—outward, upward to a better society; no rest stops to contemplate alternative routes or detours, no pauses to question goals or the means of achieving them. Building a better road has been just as natural to man as the building of a dam is to a beaver or the making of honey to a bee. The beaver society is better off for its dams and the bees (and flowers and all of nature) are better off for their honey. And few would deny that man has produced a far more rewarding society with his ever-improving transportation system.

Today man must pause. For the first time in history, ecological factors are forcing man to look critically at what he has fashioned, not with an eye toward destroying it or retarding the progress that has been man's badge of merit, but with a view toward improving it. For civilization—with all of its wonders and all of its benefits—carries within it the seeds of its own destruction. Pollution poisons our Garden of Eden, and we must find ways to keep the garden a proper paradise.

This examination will explore the possible effects of a rapidly deteriorating environment on the ability of people to enjoy the undeniable benefits of this modern society. These benefits are linked solidly with man's ability to distribute the tremendous variety of goods and products from one end of the country to the other.

Pollution and ecology—words hardly used a few short years ago—today are part of practically everybody's everyday language. A fast-growing population that has concentrated itself for the most part in relatively small densely packed areas, combined with a super-abundance of a myriad of things—necessities and luxuries—has produced a number of after-effects lumped together under the name "pollution."

This pollution of our air, our streams, our landscape, is a concern of marketing and that particular phase of marketing we call transportation. For people have to move within our cities and out of them, and goods must flow from point of origin and manufacture to wholesaler and retailer and consumer. And transportation, itself, is a major industry, dealing in terms of billions of passengers, billions of ton-miles and tens of billions of dollars.

Speaking only of transportation's effect on the city, Secretary of Transportation John A. Volpe recently said, "And we must get it in our heads once and for all that transportation is a utility which determines the effectiveness of schools,

Transportation
and
Ecology

hospitals, job training and employment accessibility. Transportation can make or break our cities as they evolve into regional urban complexes."

In country and in suburb, on the farm and in the manufacturing plant, in New York City and in Chapin, Iowa, transportation is a vital service. Society, as we know it, cannot long survive without a modern transportation system.

So when we say "marketing" is at a crossroads, we mean we all are at a crossroads. Man must now decide which road he will take to lead him out of the morass of pollution that threatens him.

Who is responsible for that pollution? We all are! Everyone who contributes to the gunk in our rivers, the smoke and gases in our air, the trash around us. All of us!

We demand our automobiles, to the tune of 25,000 new cars a day, a figure that will almost double by the end of the decade. We demand—and it is a natural demand—enough electricity to light our homes and power our television sets, air conditioners, washing machines, dishwashers, dryers, and all the other luxuries of this modern age. We demand, and get, enough power to emit about 25 million tons of polluting sulphur dioxide and oxides of nitrogen into the air. *And our demand is ever-increasing.*

All the goods and products that make ours the most affluent age in history, plus all the boxes, bottles, cans and plastics they come in, give us more waste material than we can dispose of. We generate—each and every one of us, according to a recent article in The New York Times—7 pounds of trash a day, for a coast-to-coast total of 700,000 tons! America's annual trash heap includes 6 million scrapped cars and another million trucks and buses, 30 million tons of waste paper, 48 to 55 billion discarded cans, 28 billion bottles and jars, and 100 million rubber tires weighing a million tons!

What to do? There are those who would have us stop the world. And this is one road man could conceivably take: Retreat. In order to be effective, we would have to go back 100 years, when the standard of living for the average American was well below the 1970 poverty line, and when even a high school education was for only the fortunate few. Many of us would find the life extremely hard and uncomfortable, and few could adapt to it.

Very few, indeed, would be willing to give up their automobiles—even if this were the panacea for our environmental ills. This was pointed up by two nation-wide surveys in 1967 that posed this question in terms intentionally unflattering to the automobile: "The auto pollutes air, creates traffic, demolishes property, and kills people. Is the contribution the auto makes to our way of life worth this?'' Four out of five of those answering, including those in crowded cities, answered yes.

So the road back into time—to a 72-hour work week and the wooden plow, to a life polluted by disease, overwork, and under-compensation—is an undesirable cop-out—even if it were feasible. And we must look for other routes to follow, for we must believe that a technology that has carried man to the moon and, in a sense, has enabled all of us to go along can also come up with cures for its own ailments.

An Examination: The Primary Cause

Pollution springs from affluence. The problem of garbage and trash disposal was not born of a slum environment but of an affluent one. A spewing smoke stack signals not decay, but thriving production. Man's horseless carriage is not a step backward, but a miracle in motion.

Just a very few years ago, few people were concerned about pollution. There is reason for this: A few years ago, pollution did not hang heavy over man's head.

What has happened in just these few years to bring about a general public alarm reminiscent of the anxiety that gripped Europe in the days of the Black Plague of the 14th Century?

What has happened, Edwin L. Dale, Jr., points out in a recent article in The New York Times Magazine, is what he calls "the law of compound interest." In 1957, Dale writes, the Gross National Product was $453 billion. In 1969—just 13 years later—it was, in constant dollars, $728 billion—an increase of 60 percent! And in the next 13 years, experts tell us, the GNP will rise more than $500 billion!

"This is the law of compound interest," Dale says. "These are not numbers; they are tin cans and smoke and auto exhaust. There is no visible escape from it. Applying the same percentage growth to a larger base every year, we have reached the point where our growth in one year is half the total output of Canada, fully adjusting for inflation. Another dizzying and rather horrifying way of putting it is that the real output of goods and services in the United States has grown as much since 1950 as it grew in the entire period from the landing of the Pilgrims in 1620 up to 1950."

A Fortune Magazine article treats the same phenomenon in terms of a "mass-and-energy" nimbus that surrounds each and every person in the United

States. This nimbus is made up of all the paper, plastics, scrap, ash, soot, dust, and other products and byproducts of our affluent age—2½ billion tons of material, or nearly 13 tons per person, a year, according to one estimate.

"The three million high-technology U.S. farmers put more adverse pressure on their land and rivers," Fortune says, "than the 150 million low-productivity peasant families of China put upon their land and rivers."

The population explosion, of and by itself, is not responsible for pollution. In a real sense, pollution has resulted from a most worthy enterprise—raising the standard of living. A greatly expanded population with a much lower standard of living would not be fouling the nest nearly as much as we are with our relatively high-living society.

The distribution of that population, with more and more people taking up less and less acreage, does contribute in great measure to our environmental problems. Our cities have grown along our waterways and then our railroad lines, because of the need for transportation services. Motor transportation has freed man somewhat from the need to band together at a predetermined point to take advantage of the transportation services available. How this change will affect the life of metropolitan centers as we know them is a point to be considered later in this report.

Not wishing to retreat to the grimness of a bygone era, man could take a blind road straight ahead, with no changes and a "pollution be damned" attitude. This notion is as disturbing as the destroying of the system willfully by a retreat. Pollution is a major threat that must be faced up to and overcome if we are to leave our descendants with something more than a wasteland.

CO, SO₂, and Beer Cans, Too

One thousand acres of towering ponderosa pine trees were recently cut down in the San Bernardino Mountains in California because they were dying—victims of smog. Experts say that in the San Bernardino National Forest alone, an estimated 96,000 of a total of 160,000 acres have suffered from moderate to severe smog damage.

And these trees represent only a fraction of the damage to vegetation from smog in California alone. In New Jersey, crop damage has been reported in every county. Eighteen other states also have suffered smog damage to farms and gardens.

In London, in Los Angeles, and other points both large and small, severe

5

smog accumulations have caused illness to human beings—and even death.

What has caused our air to be so foul? Particulates and gases thrown off by man's power machines. Particulates include fly ash (unburnable mineral fractions of ordinary coal), soot (burnable but unburned carbon), and lead (unburnable additive in gasoline). Gases include sulphur dioxide (SO_2), a product of the combustion of coal or oil that contains sulphur, and carbon monoxide (CO), emitted when insufficient oxygen is present during combustion in gasoline-powered internal-combustion engines. In addition, various oxides of nitrogen are produced when combustion takes place at very high temperatures, and a great many hydrocarbon compounds, particulates, and gases result from incomplete combustion.

Sulphur dioxide, a voluminous byproduct of most electric power generating plants and other coal-burning stations, has done most of the damage to materials and much of the damage to agriculture and plant life. It also has been implicated as the major cause of serious pollution incidents.

Every second, it has been estimated, about two million gallons of sewage and other fluid wastes pour into our waterways. The supply of drinking water in many parts of the country is threatened. In 1967, President Johnson said that "every major river system in the country is polluted."

Every day, every person in the United States adds to a growing trash pile. Included is the solid trash that just won't burn, corrode quickly or go away: Beer cans, soft drink cans, plastic containers, disposable bottles, all those things that just seem to collect and now are being lumped together as "the third pollution."

Noise—which is estimated to have doubled in the last generation and costs the United States, according to the World Health Organization, $4 billion a year in accidents, absenteeism, inefficiency, and compensatory payments—is another form of pollution. So is ugliness—from unsightly gaps in mountainsides due to strip mining to tree-lined country lanes cluttered with beer cans and other trash. The problem is manifold. And each aspect of pollution is somehow linked with the other. Polluted air results from more electric power which is necessary to run more and more appliances, which are a result of more and more production, which raises the standard of living while fouling up the air and water, while the higher standard of living gives people more things, which result in more trash, etc.

The problem is so complex that there are no easy solutions. What appears to be a solution today may be just another problem tomorrow. Taking garbage out to sea and dumping it sounds fine until the same garbage washes back to pollute a beach. For a time San Francisco considered hauling its refuse into the desert—until conservationists pointed out this was only moving pollution from one pile to another.

The overall dilemma is much like the one facing the builder who signed a contract to construct a new schoolhouse in a small New England town. The fine print in the contract said he had to use materials from the old school building to build the new school. But the fine print also said there would be no interruption to classes, which would continue in the old building until the new one was ready!

Electric utility companies have spent more than $1 billion on trying to control air pollution, a good part of it for mechanical and electrostatic precipitators for removing particulate matter, and many millions more on maintaining and improving water quality. Many electric companies have put up tall stacks, but their effectiveness is being questioned. Tall stacks in Britain, for example, apparently have given the Scandinavian countries across the North Sea sulphuric acid in their rain and snow.

The cheapest method for removing SO_2 before it gets into the atmosphere involves injection of limestone into the furnace, but the result is calcium sulphate —large quantities of it that are a waste disposal problem and could also be a serious water-pollution problem.

Other methods for removing SO_2 are much more costly but result in sulphur and sulfuric acids as byproducts. These can be sold to offset the cost, but in time would become a surplus on the market. Even now, producers of sulphur are extracting 21 million tons a year, while another 16 million tons are going up the chimney.

And those who feel electric engines are the answer to automobile pollution might stop to question the source of the vastly increased electric power that would be required were batteries to be charged from electrical lines. This would demand more power from generating plants. The obvious result: Just another form of pollution. One possibility is a so-called "hybrid" vehicle that would use an electric engine in town and an internal-combustion engine that would recharge the batteries in open country. But electric engines and steam engines to seriously challenge the internal-combustion engine have not yet come forth.

The Road of Improved Technology

"We have taken steps to abate aircraft noise, both now and in the future. We have won agreement from the airlines that smoke from jet engines will be cut back by 1972, not by 1974 as they had originally planned. We have supported projects to find workable new sources of propulsion for cars, trucks and buses, such as steam, electric and turbine engines. We worked closely with Detroit to get agreement on producing engines that would not require leaded gasoline. And we tightened emission standards for 1970 cars and began regulating truck and bus exhaust for the first time."

These words by Secretary of Transportation John A. Volpe before the National Press Club in Washington on March 17, 1970, may be a bit optimistic in tone, but they do point up a growing government interest in the problem. Industry, for quite some time, has been charting and putting into effect anti-pollution programs of its own. Government, a vital and welcome partner in the overall environmental campaign, is not equipped to do the job alone. We cannot legislate pollution out of existence. On the other hand, practical standards of control in keeping with technological capabilities, may well be the answer when linked with vigorous efforts of industry itself.

"There is no question that the emission standards now on the books will significantly reduce the amount of pollutants discharged to the atmosphere," says Dr. John T. Middleton, Commissioner of the National Air Pollution Control Administration, a Department of Health, Education, and Welfare office created by the Clean Air Act of 1967.

"In my judgment," Middleton says, "the best we can expect from the standards now in effect is that hydrocarbon and carbon monoxide emissions will dip in 1980 to approximately 60 percent of current emissions. . . . After that, when these standards have passed the saturation point of their effectiveness, and as vehicle use continues to increase, the levels of pollution will resume their upward climb.

"We cannot in good faith, then, report that we are winning the war with motor vehicle pollution. Rather, we are engaged in a holding action."

Still, a holding action may be said to be better than no action at all. It is allowing man to check and even reduce air pollution while his engineers and technicians work on more permanent solutions.

The new government standards also call for a minimum amount of smoke from diesel engines. Diesels do not emit toxic pollutants, according to engineers, but when they smoke, they *look like* they are polluting the air.

"Well, the diesel smoke problem, though that smoke is not toxic, must be regarded as a serious one," says Tom Head, Vice President of Research and Engineering for Cummins Engine Company, maker of truck diesels. "That is because, so far as the public is concerned, smoky trucks are a major source of trouble and are very obvious to everybody in the United States. That being the case, we must commit ourselves pretty well to the elimination of smoke as a source of nuisance."

Smoking—and noisy engines, too—are of great concern to truck manufacturers and truck users alike. While manufacturers are working on the problem on their end, conscientious motor carriers are doing their bit by use of proper fuel and regular, efficient maintenance.

But while industry is doing much to combat its environmental ills, it recognizes that large-scale effectiveness will demand Federal guidelines.

"Many people wonder why a company that owes its existence to the internal-combustion engine would favor the establishment of regulations to control emissions for these engines," says Cummins Engine Company. "The explanation is simple—government regulations are the only available means to counteract the strong competitive forces that work against the control of air pollution. Today's enlightened managements would like to do so, but it would markedly reduce their ability to compete in the market place."

Even so, private industry has made some moves on its own. As has been mentioned, electric utilities have spent $1 billion trying to clean up the air around them. Industry's expenditures in cleaning water have risen from $45 million in 1952 to an annual current rate of about $600 million.

United States Steel Corporation, a pioneer in the use of electrostatic precipitators on open hearth furnaces in the early '50s, has spent and committed a quarter of a billion dollars for pollution control over the past 10 years. Over the next few years, the company expects to commit an average of a million dollars a week for new pollution control equipment, plus a great deal more by way of research and engineering to advance the state of pollution control technology.

In three years, from 1966 to 1969, Armco Steel spent $74 million in air and water treatment facilities for its plants in Ohio, Kentucky, Missouri, Texas, and elsewhere, and its budget for maintenance of these facilities is now up to $8½ million. Bethlehem, Republic, and other steel companies also have invested heavily in pollution control, while other industries, too, have either invested, or have plans for investment, in a cleaner environment.

But money for these purposes does not grow on trees, not even for steel companies. "The dollars we put into this area are a precious commodity, just like air and water and land," says Edwin H. Gott, Chairman of U.S. Steel. "They must be deducted from the total amount we have to invest in new opportunities for growth and to improve U.S. Steel's competitive strength."

The situation is one that invites government controls. Otherwise, the corporation that spends money on pollution control will be at a tremendous disadvantage in competition with the corporation that does not.

One suggestion calls for a pollution tax, whereby each factory would pay to the extent it pollutes, with the money collected ear-marked for anti-pollution programs.

More and more government control in the whole area of environmental balance may be expected. As Fortune Magazine puts it:

"Better handling of the environment is going to require lots of legal innovation to shape the integrative forums and regulatory bodies where our new-found environmental concerns may be given concrete reality. The new legal devices will extend all the way from treaties forbidding oil pollution on the high seas down to the minute concerns of local government."

Agreements between various local and state jurisdictions may be needed to overcome another problem, one that is already interfering with the disposal of solid wastes—psychological resistance. Solid wastes, along with other trash and garbage, are being used for some rather innovative landfill operations. Using this technique—burying untreated waste in layers, each then covered by several inches of compacted earth—thousands of desolate acres have been transformed into parks, playgrounds, golf courses, bathing beaches, marinas, parking areas, and other attractive and useful areas. For example, next winter skiers are expected to be cavorting down a man-made mountain in DuPage County, Illinois, dubbed affectionately "Mount Trashmore." It is being made out of garbage. It is growing out of an unsightly marshy pit known as "The Badlands," and is taking care of the county's waste disposal problem.

But it is the county's own garbage that is forming Mount Trashmore. Apparently, *that* does make a difference. Richard D. Vaughan, Director of the Bureau of Solid Waste Management in the Department of Health, Education, and Welfare, says there is a wonderful idea making the rounds—take all the garbage and trash from the big cities where space is at a premium and haul it to the areas made desolate by strip mining. Using the land-fill technique, these areas then could be restored to their natural beauty. The trouble is, Vaughan says, the people living in the strip mine areas don't want city garbage.

In Western Pennsylvania and Maryland and upstate New York, communities which gladly use their own garbage for land-fill operations refused the refuse of Philadelphia, Baltimore, and New York—even though they could have used it.

Empty cans, throw-away bottles, old automobiles, plastic containers, toys and other objects of non-recyclable materials—all contribute to a gigantic disposal problem that will have to be solved through the technological know-how that produced them in the first place.

It is beginning to happen. New and exciting ways of recycling and re-using steel, lead, copper, brass, aluminum, paper, zinc and glass are being developed into a multi-billion dollar business.

Technology already has produced an edible film, made from a corn derivative, that could serve as the inner-liner for food packages. You just throw it in the pot with the food. It is cooked and disappears, a characteristic that might make it suitable for other kinds of packaging as well.

Industrial Designer Jerome Gould is working on a glass bottle that melts when broken, while Dr. Samuel F. Hulbert of Clemson University is working on an evaporating glass bottle.

Incineration, provided smoke and pollutants can be controlled, still might be the best answer for burnable trash. In some places—Paris, Milan (Italy), and Montreal, to name three—incinerators are the heat source for electricity generating plants. Also, it is possible to retrieve from the incinerators bits of valuables —small amounts of gold and silver, iron and aluminum—which can add up to a worthwhile return.

A Japanese scientist, Dr. Kunitoshi Tezuka, has discovered a constructive use for trash. He has a machine that compresses refuse into cubes from which are made asphalt—or concrete—coated building blocks.

So there are signs that technology may find answers to the most pressing problems of air, water, earth and noise pollution. But there remains still another

11

grave environmental situation, and it further complicates the crossroads puzzle which marketing and transportation must solve. It concerns the consumer—man himself—as it measures his ever-increasing number and his need for room in which to live, work and play.

Man: Where He Lives and Works

Man has come a long, long way in a very short time —once he got started. And where man is located now—physically and literally—is of primary importance. For it goes without saying that marketing—from production to consumption—depends on where the consumers are. As far back as 20 years ago, in the immediate postwar exodus to the suburbs, large department stores, realizing that Mohammed indeed would have to go to the mountain, began building outside the central city.

The motor vehicle—car and truck—has freed man from virtually a total dependence on the city. But as the population has moved out, the open spaces have filled in, with the result that today we have giant urban sprawls.

The urban sprawl now has reached a point where the suburbs of yesterday are wondering if they should put on the brakes. Fairfax County, just outside of Washington, D.C., has grown since World War II from a "real country" area of 70,000 persons to an urban complex of 450,000. Recently, the Fairfax County Board of Supervisors put a temporary moratorium on new construction, and was, at this writing, considering whether to make the halt indefinite. The county's water and sewage treatment facilities were being severely taxed.

Other areas, too, are feeling the environmental pinch, and are taking a hard look at the old concept that growth is good for a community. And there is no relief in sight. In the next 30 years, 100 million more persons will be occupying the land in the United States, and most of them—if projections are correct—will be occupying the land around the cities—about 8 percent of the total acreage.

Immediately following World War II, Suburbia beckoned to middle-class America with its promise of fresh air, ample room, and lovely landscape, made easily available by a housing boom coupled with ready and easy financing, including the GI Bill. But that was 50 million persons ago. Since that time, a whole generation has grown up and begun a new generation, while the exodus from the city goes on. New suburban houses are being sold in the United States at a rate of 700,000 a year.

Transportation
and
Ecology

The result is an over-crowding of Suburbia, as evidenced by what some feel is a new concept in suburban living—the town house, the suburban high-rise, and other multi-unit dwellings—all borrowed from the inner city, dressed up, and given new names.

Asks William J. Levitt, builder of mass housing developments: "Where will I ever find another potato field within commuting distance of a city?"

That would depend on what you call the city. What is happening is that the immense jam of people and vehicles that has been part of the city for years is now spreading outward, so that what were once satellite suburbs now are part of a teeming urban complex. "The great threat that now faces us," reads the report of the President's Task Force on Rural Development, "is that the social and economic ills of the nation's inner cities may worsen and spread over entire urban areas, infecting the entire national structure unless we act together with intelligence to prevent it. Even now, 70 percent of our people are jammed onto 2 percent of the Nation's land. But if present trends continue, by the year 2000 more than 174 million people will be huddled in cities concentrated in five small geographic areas."

Meanwhile, plans to pump new life into cities continue, with rapid mass transit systems getting priority treatment in many urban centers, and with new office buildings changing the skylines in cities throughout the country. New York is enjoying its greatest growth in office space in history. Last year, 18 new buildings, with a total office space of 16,150,000 square feet, sprang up in Manhattan—a record. Add 15 million square feet of office space this year, and 27 million more next year, and it is clear that New York is far from an expiration date.

Those office buildings will need people. And as the population and the number of autos, trucks, and buses rise (some say motor vehicles will number 170 million by 1985, a 60 percent increase over today's figure), there will be a continuing clogging of the arteries in the metropolitan areas. By the end of this decade, traffic volume in the metropolitan area of Pittsburgh is expected to be up 40 percent; in Boston, up 50 percent; in Detroit, 90 percent, and Los Angeles, 100 percent.

Inner-cities already are bursting at the seams with traffic. And yet, transportation—commercial and passenger—will determine whether our system of urban living will continue to work. The time may come when both the truck and automobile will be banned from the cities during certain hours. In 1962, Tokyo

13

put a ban on large commercial vehicles on main streets during daylight hours. This is not exactly a new idea. Julius Caesar once banned freight carts from the streets of Rome during daylight hours because they were clogging up the streets. But like many so-called solutions to transportation problems, that just created another problem for Caesar: The traffic at night kept everybody awake!

People, as well as vehicles, may be restricted from certain areas, according to some observers. Sam Studebaker, the former President of the National Association of Soil and Water Conservation Districts, sees a time when U.S. citizens will need a permit to live in certain areas.

Marketing—the very lifeline of our civilization—depends upon free and easy transportation from producer to consumer. With the advent of suburban living, marketing had to undergo changes in order to service those new and growing communities. One result was the shopping center—a complex of retail shops and stores, with large parking areas. Often, these centers feature branches of old, established inner-city department stores. With the population shifts from inner-city to Suburbia, many of the mother stores have experienced a downhill slide, while the branches have known a continuous rise.

These shopping centers, of course, have been geared to a mobile consumer, who commutes 10, 15, 20 and more miles to work, drives to a bank window and deposits part of his paycheck without getting out of his car, and wheels to his favorite shopping center to stock up on needs and little luxuries.

Highways have made it all possible and the nation has done a tremendous job of roadbuilding in the past 15 years. More is in the works, but not enough. As Secretary of Transportation Volpe points out, new vehicles are being added to the roads at such a rate that highway construction cannot keep up "by any stretch of the dollar or the imagination."

Perhaps—and some hold this to be very likely—the clogged urban complexes will not remain confined to today's geographic limits, expanding like balloons to the bursting point, but will move ever outward and may give birth to a whole flock of separate towns and small cities.

The beltways, which surround a good many cities, seem to favor this idea of growth. Detroit, for example, has a series of such concentric rings helping to link the inner-city with areas of greater and greater distance from it, as well as dispersing through traffic. Certainly one may expect both industrial and residential growth to follow such highway building, for this has been the pattern.

Transportation
and
Ecology

A move outward to what is now the rural areas is the primary recommendation of the 49-page Presidential study group report mentioned previously. The report calls for better job opportunities in rural areas, and proposes a massive effort by private enterprise, with support from the government, "to create more economic opportunities and a better environment in countryside America."

Specifically, the study group urged tax incentives for companies locating in designated "rural development areas," and a "Rural Development Credit Bank" to provide funds for housing, sewage, and other needs.

The Task Force also called for highway development in rural areas. "Efficient transportation is basic to an easy, rapid flow of resources into and out of countryside areas," the report reads. "It greatly increases the mobility of labor through 'people-to-job' roads; it promotes dispersal of industry and counteracts the economic and social ills of urban compaction; it improves the quality of living and the environment for residents; and it gives people access to open space and recreation.

"The Task Force recommends that the Federal Highway Act be amended to provide for a classification in the Federal-State highway system to be designated 'rural development highways.' These new short-mileage highways should lead to existing highways, thereby serving local areas that have a high development potential."

Satellite cities and towns—separate from the urban complex but within reasonable commuting distance from it (nowadays 50 miles is considered reasonable by many)—could be the major remedy for the concentration of people in the large metropolitan centers. These satellites—made possible by the motor vehicles and modern highways—already are a reality. They include planned, virtually self-contained communities, such as Reston, Virginia, and Columbia, Maryland, and old towns that have been brought into the city's sphere of influence by highway development.

Also a reality are industrial parks—towns for working only—which prove you can take the office and plant out of the city. Not only do these parks relieve inner-city congestion on their own, but they also induce residential building in areas relatively nearby.

But, as the Task Force report indicates, natural and voluntary development of rural sectors may not be sufficient to give the cramped, overtaxed urban complexes meaningful relief. Help from the government may well be necessary.

15

Marketing, of course, will change with a diffusion of the population. Truck terminal facilities, located in areas where there is ample room, benefit both shippers and carriers—and, ultimately, consumers. Automation, the most advanced freight handling techniques, and ample dock space for receiving and shipping are used to minimize time and expense, and numerous bays for loading and unloading have meant a much smoother flow of traffic.

Industry has similarly shortened the order-delivery cycle by locating distribution centers in strategic locations and thus replacing a dozen or more warehouses and numerous offices throughout the country. One can see where one distribution center, or manufacturing plant, or warehouse, centrally located, could service five so-called satellite cities with greater economy and efficiency than could one facility in the innards of the central city miles away, or five small facilities, one in each of the satellite cities.

On the other hand, there are those who see for man not an expansion of his living space, but a contraction. One such view is offered by Architect Paolo Soleri, a former student of Frank Lloyd Wright, who envisions mile-high cities built on water and on land. These cities would be highly efficient and complex, as Soleri sees them, with the residents neatly packed in layer on top of layer, as many as 2.4 million persons in one such towering beehive.

Soleri calls his sea cities "Novanaohs" and says they would rest on high buoyancy canisters and would be made primarily of corrosion-resistant steel. He calls his land cities "Babel" cities, after the Biblical tower.

These cities in the air, whether resting on land or sea, would need a tremendous transportation area just to get the goods in and the waste material out. The marketing logistics alone are staggering. For example, how many tractor trailers would be needed to get one day's supply of breakfast food alone to the ground level of such a sardine-can skyscraper? How many giant elevators would be needed to keep the goods flowing from ground level to the upper areas?

While Soleri may be dreaming of a distant day, at least one organization already has laid down plans for a similar project. The project, called the Jonathan Housing Corporation, has plans for a new kind of experimental community near Minneapolis. "It plans to build homes based on the 'stack' concept—that is, constructing finished living modules and stacking them around a central stair core," reads an ad in The New York Times by one of the participating companies. "Essentially," the ads says, "the community is a city in embryo, with five semi-independent villages (or neighborhoods) surrounding a town center, which will consist of a single, large multi-purpose building built over the railroad and principal highway."

One unit would be stacked on top of another—apartment houses on hospitals, playgrounds on supermarkets on garages.

While these are interesting concepts, one would have to say that at this stage in man's history, people preferences seem to point in the opposite direction. Man seems to like the free-wheeling mobility made possible by the motor vehicle. The tendency in living quarters today—town houses in the country, satellite cities, sprawling motels as opposed to skyscraping hotels—seems to be away from the tight urban complex.

Transportation à la Mode

One thing that will be essential for the efficient transportation of goods in an ever-expanding economy and for a meaningful attack on man's environmental problems is the fullest utilization of the various modes. As Secretary Volpe puts it: "We can no longer make do with mere transportation 'networks,' each spinning on its own merry way. We must create a balanced, harmonious transportation system that meets a number of pressing social needs."

The efficient movement of people and goods will necessarily be dependent on a growing capability among all modes and, certainly such growth is indicated. Projections to 1980 show motor carriers, railroads, airways, pipelines and inland water carriers all earning substantial increases in revenue. Motor carriers, in addition to their capability of complete transportation services alone, will play a vital role in increases gained by other modes because almost all freight must first be hauled to the other modes, and then from them to an ultimate destination, by trucks. Recent projections indicate that within 30 years the increase in highway freight will require 2½ times the number of trucks and combinations that are on the road today.

For long distance movement of freight a growing dependence on aircraft is a certainty. Super airports, capable of handling the larger jets, have already begun to appear—in Houston, in Tampa, in Kansas City. Louisville plans a new international airport capable of accommodating both SST's and subsonic jets, while plans have been proposed for a $530 million floating air-seaport 30 miles

17

off New York in the Atlantic Ocean. This amazing facility, if it ever materializes, will have 14 runways, one two miles long and 300 feet wide, docking space for 480 ships, plus office buildings, warehouses, and a large hotel—all located on a large floating steel slab!

Already operating is the so-called jumbo jet, which can carry in its belly alone almost as much cargo as a normal-sized jet freighter can carry fully loaded, with no passengers.

Meanwhile, work progresses on aircraft with minimum space capability for taking off and landing (STOL, for short takeoff and landing), and on craft capable of vertical takeoff and landing (VTOL). One VTOL craft, the helicopter, has proved itself of cargo-handling value in Vietnam and is expected to be used more in this country in supporting transportation operations. "At least a dozen companies have various types of helicopters with varying horsepower, gross weights, useful loads, range and speed, either operational, in progress or under development," reports a recent issue of U.S. Transport Magazine.

Certainly, helicopters may be expected to offer quick relief in emergency situations. For example, experiments have shown that the giant whirlybirds can be used to transport cargo from ships standing idly by because of overcrowded docks. Such an operation could reduce "down time" (time when equipment operations are interrupted)—the horror of all transport people—and keep ships productively under way.

Railroads have put new life into their freight operations with such modern advances as centralized traffic control, push-button yards, ever-larger cars, and the unit train—an entire train set up to haul just one product, thus facilitating movement and minimizing handling. For fast, overland transportation of people, perhaps the tracked air cushion vehicle may provide an answer. The Grumman Aerospace Corporation recently was awarded a contract by the Department of Transportation to design such a vehicle capable of speeds up to 300 miles per hour.

Intercontinental shipping has been vastly improved with containerization and accommodating port facilities, while the inland water system is keeping pace, too. New navigation techniques and equipment have been developed to permit around-the-clock operations of towing vessels in all kinds of weather. Today, 38 of the 50 states, claiming almost 95 percent of the population, have commercial transportation services provided by vessels operating on 25,000 miles of rivers, canals, bays, sounds and lakes. Radical new designs give promise of improved travel over these inland waterways. Hydrofoils—basically jet-propelled ships on stilts—and hovercraft—vessels that cruise on an air cushion over water and land—are among the more exciting vehicles on the horizon.

Pipelines, once used to carry oil products exclusively, now are in the midst of technological advances also. An 850-mile line now carries a fertilizer, anhydrous ammonia, from Texas to the farming areas of Iowa. A 273-mile line has begun to carry coal to a generating plant in Nevada. A San Francisco corporation has found a way to condense iron ore into a powdery mixture and pump it through pipes. (Experimenters have found that most things that can be reduced to a powder can be mixed with a liquid, usually water, sent through pipes and restored to their natural dry state at the other end.) Now engineers and chemists are working on reducing other bulk commodities to this "slurry" condition and also are experimenting with containers (hollow steel or aluminum cylinders, soft plastic bags, etc.) that may lend themselves to this imaginative concept of getting goods to market.

The efficient flow of goods by air and rail, water and pipeline, must necessarily depend on the efficiency of the flow of the goods to and from the terminals serving these modes. In most cases, the motor truck provides that invaluable service.

Intermodal efficiency has, of course, been greatly enhanced by containerization and new advances in this area are on the way. One may look for improvements, too, in shipping containers. Standard, protective two-way containers might well make obsolete today's packaging that is thrown away after one use and thus adds to the disposal problem while necessitating excessive handling.

The Long View

Visionaries can see a time when powerful, fast-moving tractor-trailer combinations will haul freight over super highways, be broken into smaller units off the super highways, and even smaller units for distributing goods in urban areas.

George F. Butts, Product Planning Manager and Chief Engineer at Dodge Truck Operations, sees a unit that would never leave the intercontinental highway. It would be capable of continuous operation on a 24-hour, around-the-clock basis.

19

"The power requirements for these future highway machines could necessitate the development of power plants not yet conceived," Butts theorizes. "It may even be that these trucks of the future will be guided and controlled by an electronic guidance system coast to coast.

"This tractor of the future may have a cab interior that provides the comforts of home, including washroom, cooking area, lounge, and sleeping facilities."

As with other modes, the motor carrier industry is relying more and more on computers and other electronic marvels to facilitate the handling and shipment of goods, particularly in terminal facilities. Handling & Shipping Magazine recently looked into the crystal ball and saw this change in transferring shipments at a motor carrier terminal:

"The driver, having positioned the trailer or container at the dock, connects the floor-mounted conveyor in the trailer to the terminal conveyor system, and presses a button. The freight unloads automatically, electric sensors read coded markings on the packages as they enter the system. The LTL shipments move through the terminal complex, are weighed and cubed electronically, as the conveyor takes the freight to an assigned staging area for unitization."

Highways and streets of the future also will make use of electronics to make them safer and more efficient. Traffic jams on the Chicago freeways have been alleviated by the use of control units that advise motorists to adjust their speed well in advance of jams, while at an intersection in Buffalo, television cameras are recording all kinds of pertinent information, including the causes of collisions.

Highway dangers and nuisances, such as rail grade crossings and poorly drained road surfaces, will be eliminated in the future, while chemical treatment of the roads to prevent icing will be commonplace, according to ICC Commissioner Rupert L. Murphy.

Somewhere in man's future, dreamers say, will be pipelines that will carry people as well as all manner of goods; moving sidewalks that will eliminate the need for passenger vehicles in the cities, and rockets that will carry passengers from America to Europe in minutes!

Look far enough ahead and you may see interplanetary travel, which—if presently in vogue—would afford a wonderful relief for the environmental pressures that plague us. But man has to come up with some relief today if he is going to be around for journeying to Mars tomorrow!

The relief may well include new engines and new fuels. It may, indeed, as

Transportation
and
Ecology

some have suggested, include a shorter work week, so as to reduce the growth rate of the Gross National Product, and thus diminish the "mass and energy" nimbus around each of us—a nimbus that includes, among other things, throwaway containers, automobiles, trash, the enzymes in our detergents, and the sulphur dioxide cast into our atmosphere by the burning of coal to power all of our electrical needs.

The cure probably will include different kinds of packaging, and perhaps a purposeful elimination of certain products. "The cost will be enormous," says Richard B. Stoner, Vice Chairman of the Board of the Cummins Engine Company, "and it is likely some industries will need governmental assistance and incentives. Unfortunately, some enterprises will not survive, but that is a necessary cost."

A new source of power to replace the fossil fuels could produce an industrial and social revolution of unprecedented impact and scope. One source of power—the earth itself—has been tapped, in Iceland, Italy, New Zealand, Japan, Mexico, the Soviet Union, and, more recently, in Northern California. In 1960, the Pacific Gas and Electric Company tapped into the geothermal energy steaming up from the earth's crust in the area of the "big geysers." Since then, it has tripled its original pilot plant capacity to 82,000 kilowatts, and is expected to double the capacity again in 1972.

Half a dozen large oil companies in the United States are prospecting for geothermal wells—the technology is the same as that for obtaining oil.

Slowly, over eons and eons, the decay of radioactive elements in rocks has fired up this tremendous furnace, which breaks through the earth's crust in the form of volcanoes, geysers, hot springs, and steam vents known as fumaroles.

Just below the surface of the United States there is enough heat stored to a depth of six miles to replace 900 trillion tons of coal! Cooling the earth's center by just one degree Fahrenheit, experts say, would release enough heat energy to run all the existent power plants for 20 million years.

But, of course, the "hot spots" near the earth's surface—where this power is currently available—are scattered, and this power source, like oil and coal, must be sought-after, discovered, and harnessed. Perhaps in time, technology will permit the drilling farther down—to the more intense heat sources.

Geothermal power is still an insignificant energy source, with only about one million kilowatts being generated worldwide, but experts say it could in time

21

rival—or surpass—all other electrical power sources, including nuclear energy.

Nuclear energy—in its present stage—is not the blessing some had hoped it would be. It causes thermal pollution of water, and is expensive. Moreover, there is concern over availability of fuel sources. The development of the breeder reactor—which actually creates more fissionable fuel than it consumes—could solve the fuel problem, but the reactor is not perfected. In addition, expensive and complex safeguards will be required, thus keeping the cost of electricity high.

Nuclear fusion—the joining of atoms, as opposed to splitting of atoms as in fission—could end all of man's power problems in one magnificent breakthrough. However, no one can predict when the big breakthrough will occur, thus eliminating—for all time—man's worry about sources of power.

Conclusion

Man has traveled a far piece—both figuratively and literally—and in the journey has encountered a myriad of obstacles, countless threats, scores of crises; some of his own making, some just dealt out to him in the natural course of events.

In his movement outward and upward from the grubby hardships of a primitive life, man has learned to corral and domesticate fowl and cattle, has dammed rivers and has taken his roads over and through mountains; has conquered diseases once ascribed to the power of Satan; has written great books and played lilting music; has split the atom and has planted his feet on a glowing sphere 250,000 miles in the sky.

With a horizontal opposed thumb, a fertile brain, and a largess from Heaven unlimited in abundance and wonder, man has explored, experimented, and expanded his horizons, and has fashioned for himself a life that gives promise of excitement, comfort, and fulfillment in a way the dreams of his ancestors could barely outline.

And carrying man along this fabulous journey—from cave to spaceship—has been his transportation system and, in particular, his ability to move people and goods across farther and farther distances in greater and greater quantities in less and less time.

Man has not solved all of his problems. Wars still plague parts of his planet, while a greater conflict with self-annihilating implications hangs heavy over his head. Still, the miraculous communications network he has fashioned gives promise of an increasing dialogue among his warring tribes. Disease continues to strike down large numbers of men, indiscriminately. And yet, a list of diseases virtually conquered reads like a list of great battles in an epic war: Childbed fever, diphtheria, poliomyelitis, scarlet fever, yellow fever, smallpox. Poverty continues to be a way of life for many. But in those nations where free enterprise has been allowed free reign, the list of those so afflicted grows smaller and there is good reason to believe that poverty, like poliomyelitis, may someday rank among man's more worthy conquests.

And now man faces a new kind of threat. His power plants, machines and products, which have given him an unprecedented world of abundance, also are giving him an unprecedented abundance of pollutants. His cup runneth over, and so do his garbage dumps. His waterways are foul; his air full of smoke, sulphur dioxide, and carbon monoxide. He has too many people crammed into too-small spaces, and noise and ugliness surround him.

Man will someday cure cancer. Few persons doubt this. The reason for unbounded optimism in this battle against an ages-old enemy is simply that man recognizes the nature of the enemy. And this is the story of man's progress: Recognition of a problem, determination to solve it, and application.

And these are what man brings today to the battle against pollution. He will win that battle. It will take great sums of money, much legislation on the part of the Federal and State Governments, and cooperation among all men and all institutions. Government and industry must join hands, and the average man must join in the fight with his contribution as an individual.

Marketing, as we know it today, will surely undergo change, as man's methods of production and his manner of living undergo change. But regardless of whether tomorrow's motor carriers operate out of terminal complexes in the country and utilize electric carts in the inner-city; regardless of whether their freight includes beverages bottled in containers programmed to self-destruct 18 seconds after being emptied; regardless of whether tomorrow's railroads zip along several feet above ground at 500 m.p.h., and giant airplanes take off and land on a dime—the name of the game will remain the same: Progress. Providing the most good to the most numbers of people. A steady rise in the standard of living.

This is what Columbus sought when he crossed the Atlantic. This is what Daniel Boone went after when he carved a road out of the Kentucky wilderness.

2

Transportation
Amid
Social Change
and Crisis

Transportation
Amid
Social Change
and Crisis

Life
in a Whirl

Life, in this year of 1972, in this highly techno-logical society, is in a whirl. Never before, or so it seems, has this nation in particular—and the world in general—faced such over-powering problems, with the result that confusion reigns in place of conviction and uncertainty has replaced resolve.

Or so it seems.

This nation has faced crises before. Two world wars and a grave economic depression—shattering, indeed, at the time they occurred—are among the memories of many living citizens.

But there is something different about today's problems. For one thing, growth has made everything bigger and more complicated. And it certainly seems reasonable that we are the victims of what historian Arthur M. Schlesinger Jr. calls the "increase in the velocity of history." That simply means—and who can doubt it?—that the world is changing at a faster and faster rate, with the result that decades now see more major changes than centuries used to.

In the past two decades, for example, we have seen distances on earth sharply reduced by the advent of the jet airliner, and we have seen man soar through space and set foot on the moon. And just one decade ago, ecology was considered to be simply a branch of biology; today it is the cover word for a great assortment of horrors, all brought about—for the most part—by man and his growth.

And it goes without saying that transportation and marketing—two essentials of today's economy—must necessarily respond to all nuances of society's changes, including those changes brought about by man in the solution of his problems.

In Chapter I we explored the possible effects on transportation and marketing from man's coping with his ecological problems—the pollution of his air, his streams, and his land by his factories, his machines, his abundance of products. It was pointed out in that report that man may well have to adjust some of his methods of production, transportation, and marketing of goods in order to cope with these most serious threats to his very existence.

But what about the other vast problem area, so closely related to, but in some ways separate from, the environmental structure—the sociological framework of man's existence? How will man eventually deal with his densely populated urban complexes, a changing labor market, advancing technology, the problems of specific minority groups, and other such challenges? And how will transportation and marketing lead changes, or respond to such changes?

This chapter will explore these questions. Admittedly, there will be some overlapping with Chapter One because the subjects overlap. For example, is the population density around urban centers an ecological or a sociological problem? The answer, of course, is both. On the other hand, projected changes in the nature of the labor market—more workers in the service industries and fewer in goods producing—are strictly a sociological concern.

There will not be any vainglorious pretense at expertise in forecasting. There can be few solid predictions. What we are dealing with primarily is change, the nature of which defies the soothsayer. Rather, we will attempt to state the problems, to outline the trends, to present the alternatives, with the aim of helping you, the reader, to venture a more educated appraisal of transportation and marketing in the light of today's problems and tomorrow's possible solutions.

People: In Town and Country

Sudden, intense change is pelting man like a mysterious fallout from outer space. "A fire storm of change," former Fortune Editor Alvin Toffler calls it in his book, "Future Shock," which is all about change and its debilitating effect on man. "We have not merely extended the scope and scale of change, we have radically altered its pace," Toffler writes. "We have in our time released a totally new social force—a stream of change so accelerated that it influences our sense of time, revolutionizes the tempo of daily life, and affects the very way we 'feel' the world around us."

But this maelstrom, both magnificent and terrifying, which is now attracting the attention of such social students as Schlesinger and Toffler, is not just the result of the great leap forward in technology. One of the great, dramatic and socially traumatic changes that has been taking place quickly—and yet, in a sense, quietly, like Sandburg's fog coming on little cat feet—has been the change in our numbers. There are so many more of us in these United States—25 million more than just 10 years ago, 55 million more than 20 years ago, 130 million more than were here at the turn of the century.

Still sheer numbers do not a maelstrom make. In the census year of 1970, there were about 205 million persons in the United States, but ours is not an over-populated country in the Malthusian sense that our food supply and other necessities for life are threatened. In fact, compared to most nations, the United States—with just 57 persons per square mile—is sparsely populated. Compare that with Holland's density of 928 persons per square mile. England's population (590 persons per square mile) is 10 times as dense and Switzerland's is seven times as dense as the U.S. population.

Someone riding a crowded subway in New York may doubt it, but the truth is you could put the entire U.S. population in single-family, typical suburban homes in about half the state of Michigan.

Moreover, the growth rate of our population has been on the decline since the Civil War when it was 3 percent per year. Now it is about 1 percent per year, less than half the growth rate for the rest of the world. The fertility rate (the number of births per 1,000 women aged 15-44)—another reliable gauge for population trends—is at the lowest since the Depression. In 1936, this figure fell to 75.8, lowest since reliable record-keeping was started in the early 1900's. In 1957 —banner year for the post-World War II baby crop—the figure rose to 122.9, highest since the years immediately preceding World War I. Since then, the fertility rate has been falling—to 119 in 1960, to 87.6 in 1970.

Of course, population alarmists can point out that a decrease in rate does not mean a decrease in population, and this is true enough. But some observers actually see a stabilization of the population in the near future. That 1957 baby crop will be having its own offspring in the immediate years ahead, but the national concern over population, the emphasis on having smaller families, and the increasing knowledge and availability of birth control aids may well combine to act as a governor. In fact, Dennis H. Wrong, New York University professor and author and a recognized authority in the field of demography, foresees the possibility of a zero rate of population growth for the U.S. before the end of the century, perhaps even in the next decade.

But if we are not an overcrowded country, it sure seems as though we are. For while we have vast open spaces—more open spaces than a generation ago, according to Wrong—where people are *not* does not constitute the problem. It is where they *are* that counts. And most people today—at least 71 percent—are living in urban areas.

"How are you going to keep them down on the farm?" a World War I song asked, and the answer—then and now—is that you aren't. The exodus from country to city has been going on since the turn of the century. It is a natural exodus because, as technology increases, fewer and fewer persons are living directly off the land. At the turn of the century, Benjamin Chinitz points out in the book, "City and Suburb," 40 percent of the total work force was employed in "primary" industries—agriculture, mining, fishing, forestry and other such fields where the products are the fruits of nature in their original, or close to original, state. Now, less than 10 percent are so employed.

Take farming, that largest and most basic of the primary industries. There are about 3 million farms in the United States at the present time—about one-half the number we had just 30 years ago. Moreover, the small farm is on the way out, it seems. Farms grossing less than $10,000 have dropped from 4 million in 1939 to about 1 million today, and their share of agricultural sales has dipped from nearly 50 percent to about 15 percent.

A growing technology that has brought better machinery and more sophisticated techniques to the farm has raised productivity dramatically. In 1910, one farm worker supplied products for only seven persons. In 1970, one farm worker supplied himself and 45 other persons.

The result is that agricultural production today uses one-third as much farm labor as in 1910, though the population has more than doubled since that time.

Certainly, a major contributor to that growing technology has been automotive farm equipment including equipment designed for and tailored to the needs of specific crops, such as fruits, grains, fibers, etc. And certainly, a most important contributor to that growing technology has been the motor truck, which—in combination with modern highway development—has greatly facilitated the job of getting the produce to market. About 3½ million trucks are used today in agriculture. Modern, refrigerated trucks and highly developed storage and packaging facilities help make it possible for practically all Americans to eat in a manner available only to the extremely well-to-do in bygone years.

And what about all those people no longer tilling the soil? (In the Middle Ages it took 99 persons to produce enough food for 100, leaving one person out of 100 to work in other areas.) Today the ratio is 45 non-farm workers to 1 farm worker, a ratio that works in favor of advanced technology, the scientific fields, manufacturing of non-essential products and the service industries. And this, of course, is what has been happening.

This trend toward an increasingly more efficient use of the land will continue. By 1980, the Department of Agriculture predicts, the total number of farms may decline from 3 million to 2 million, though the area farmed will remain the same. "As much as 90 percent of all farm products marketed in 1980 may be produced by some 500,000 to 600,000 farming units," says Under Secretary of Agriculture J. Phil Campbell. "Commercial farms will be fewer, larger, and more efficiently operated. The amount of land used for agriculture will probably be about the same as today, but farmers will use much more capital and considerably less manpower."

People: In Suburbia

All the manpower released from the soil has made its way to the city. The city has been where the action is, where the jobs are. So they came to the cities, from the farms and the hamlets, to work, to marry, to raise families.

And their families grew up and married and started families of their own and something else began to happen: People—a significant number of people— began moving out of the cities. They did not go back to the farms, for their ties were now with the city. But they wanted at least a touch of rural life—a patch of green grass instead of asphalt, trees instead of street lamps, and flowerbeds instead of window boxes. They began to move to the suburbs, an exodus aided and abetted by the World War II GI housing bill, roads, and the automobile.

And then the suburbs began to spread.

Today, more than half the people living in metropolitan areas live outside the central city. It is a highly mobile population that depends almost exclusively on the motor truck to keep it supplied with all the needs and wants of modern suburban living, and on personal transportation automobiles to commute to and from the city.

And when the people moved out, commercial enterprises followed. The supermarket and the shopping center became part of everyday language.

Certainly such an expansion would have been virtually impossible without the people mobility and ease of transportation of goods and products offered by motor vehicles.

And the more populated Suburbia becomes, and the farther it spreads geographically, the greater will be the dependence on motor transportation.

The National Goals Research Staff, established by President Nixon on July 13, 1969, in its published report to the President, dated July 4, 1970, had this to say on the metropolitan spread:

"Assuming that the trends continue unabated, most of the U.S. population growth over the next few decades will be concentrated in the 12 largest urban regions. These 12 metropolitan areas occupying one-tenth of the land area will contain over 70 percent of the population. Moreover, at least 50 percent of the total population will be found in three great metropolitan belts: Boston-Washington, Chicago-Pittsburgh, San Francisco-San Diego. These three centers will include an overwhelming proportion of the most technologically advanced and the most prosperous and creative elements of the society."

As more and more people congregate in these huge, dense belts, and as the spaces within each fill up, more and more short-haul transportation will be needed. All modes—airplanes, trains and trucks—may be expected to expand their long-haul operations, providing essential transportation between these belts.

People: Growing Older

There is one sector in our population that is most important when discussing population trends—the aged among us. There are 20 million Americans 65 and over—a very significant 10 percent of the population. People in that age bracket made up only 2.5 percent of the population in 1850.

Not only are the elderly growing in numbers, but they are more independent than ever before, thanks in great measure to such social welfare programs as Social Security and Medicare and to the general rise in the standard of living. Advances in medicine, too, have increased their numbers and added to their vigor. Years ago, it was common practice for the elderly to live with and to live off their children. Today, it is more common for Grandpa and Grandma to maintain their own home. The result has been the springing up of "retirement villages"—clusters of new homes that are restricted to people in the upper age brackets and which, for the most part, are a part of the suburban growth pattern.

Not all the elderly—not even a large percentage of them—are currently housed in such homogeneous townships, but the presence of such complexes reflects the growing emergence of this group. And certainly it is a group whose demand for goods and services and increasing ability to pay for them are of significant interest to those who manufacture, transport and market such goods and services.

The elderly also must be added to the ever-growing list of those in the market for housing. The economy has curtailed house building, but an upswing apparently is now under way. To meet the country's needs under goals set by the Government, about 25 million new homes will be needed in the decade ahead. And most of those new homes, experts envision, are going to be erected in the suburban areas. It follows that these suburban areas will continue to spread, like the ripples in a pond moving ever outward from the disturbed center. And along with the new housing will be new shopping centers and other marketing and servicing enterprises, of course, totally dependent on efficient, mobile transportation of people and goods.

Decline of the City

When the preliminary reports of the 1970 census were released in mid-year, surprise was registered in cities throughout the land. Galveston, Tex.; East Lansing, Mich.; Milwaukee, Omaha, Kansas City, Birmingham, Mobile, Ala., and Alexandria, Va.—all were told their populations were considerably less than expected. Officials of some cities reacted with disbelief, even anger. Re-counts have been made, but no major errors in the original census have been uncovered, as of this writing.

Final census figures show that St. Louis had lost 17 percent of its population since 1960; Savannah, Ga., was down 20.7 percent; Youngstown, Ohio, down 16.1 percent; Camden, N.J., down 12.5 percent—to name just a few.

Some cities have gained in population, but the overall trend continues to be a movement out of the city into the suburbs. And quite naturally there has been a reaction. Aside from the financial and political repercussions inherent in such things as tax bases, federal and state aid programs and legislative representation, a population loss means a more direct financial downgrading. Businesses suffer, stores close, and the owners either retire, move their operations into the suburbs or go into some other line of endeavor.

A word is in order at this point about another of the sociological problems having a bearing on this phenomenon of flight to suburbia: Crime. The vast increase in urban crime is certainly a factor in the overall undesirability of living in the city. However, one could argue that the rise in crime is not a cause of the exodus to suburbia but a result, for as the more affluent and more educated segments of a society leave a certain area, the more susceptible that area and those left behind are to the criminal elements.

Certainly in the wake of the general exodus there is a deterioration of the inner city. Curiously there is a growing density of population of those same inner cities. This tight concentration of people in a deteriorating environment is a breeding ground for crime.

Obviously, the serious urban crime picture is a factor that must be dealt with. Our cities must be made manageable.

Those who have been in the forefront of efforts to rebuild the cities have insisted that an efficient mass transportation system is a necessity. The banning of motor vehicles—or certain kinds of motor vehicles—inside central cities has been proposed. Perhaps the day may come when the average suburbanite will need two cars: A heavy, powerful, smooth-riding automobile for long distance driving and a smaller, less powerful car for city driving.

Any mass transportation system that would eliminate or sharply curtail the use of private automobiles in downtown areas would create an increased need for pickup and delivery vehicles. "Today the stores try to make you carry as much as you can," says one observer, an executive who does a measure of downtown shopping, "but I don't mind. You only have to carry it to the parking lot and put it in your car and you have it when you get home. With mass transit, though, you will expect them to deliver it. So that is going to mean more trucks for retail delivery. Or, the alternative is to do all our shopping in the suburban areas."

The magazine, U.S. News & World Report, points up the critical situation faced by cities throughout the country. A number of these cities have been waging extensive campaigns to make their downtown areas attractive places after dark. Billions of dollars have been invested to bring back the shopper and diner,

1640964

the theater-patron and sports fan to the urban centers. More police, improved lighting and new expressways to facilitate commuting—all have been employed in what planners hope is the start of big comebacks for such cities as Los Angeles, San Francisco, Atlanta, Chicago, St. Louis, Detroit, Houston and Newark, the article reported.

What the future will bring is problematical. Certainly there are two opposing forces at work today, one operating in favor of abandonment of the city and the other working in favor of saving it. But if the city does survive, it will not be the same kind of place we have known up until now. Some observers, like the well-known Dr. Desmond Morris, say the entire concept of the city will have to be changed.

"Our cities grew up in their present form centuries ago and have never been changed," says Dr. Morris, author of a number of best-selling books on man and nature. Originally, Dr. Morris points out, cities were designed to accommodate a few thousand people. Now they contain millions, but they continue to develop along the original pattern.

"It is incredibly primitive to allow a city to swell to 100 times its original size without redesigning it. You wouldn't build a motor car 100 times its original size without a radical change in design. In our big cities we have, in effect, done just that."

Architect Paolo Soleri, once a student of Frank Lloyd Wright, says cities must eventually "miniaturize." He looks to the day when man will live in very tall (more than twice the height of the Empire State Building) complexes, densely packed at a minimum of 60 persons per acre, which is about four times the density of the population of Washington, D.C. These structures, Soleri theorizes, could be built on land, or even on the open sea, on high buoyancy canisters made of corrosion-resistant steel.

Automation would be used extensively, Soleri says, but even so, the logistics of such dwellings would be staggering. One such plan—Soleri has a number of variations which he details in his book, "City in the Image of Man,"—calls for a population of 2.4 million packed in at the rate of 345 persons to an acre. Trucking in breakfast food alone for that many people living in a "miniaturized" sky-scraping city is something to think about.

Another and similar concept is actually in the planning stage, according to a recent ad in The New York Times. Here is part of the text of that ad, sponsored by a producer of building materials:

"The only way a city can beat the population explosion is build up not out. To build apartment houses on top of hospitals, playgrounds on top of supermarkets, on top of garages. To combine facilities—like merging a nighttime theater with a daytime lecture hall, or a daytime courtroom with a nighttime classroom.

"As a step towards this change, Olin has joined with several companies in a new project called the Jonathan Housing Corporation, an experimental 'living laboratory' to test housing innovations.

"It plans to build homes based on the 'stack' concept—that is, constructing finished living modules and stacking them around a central core—in an experimental community near Minneapolis.

"Essentially, the community is a city in embryo, with five semi-independent villages (or neighborhoods) surrounding a town center, which will consist of a single, large multipurpose building built over the railroad and principal highway.

"This project will point the way to a new type of city, combining the advantages of decentralization with the advantages of centralization. It could prove the viability of the multi-purpose building as a major solution to the space problem."

Such a concept will require as a major implementation adequate facilities for the delivery of all the products and goods that will be needed to sustain the development and equally adequate and substantial disposal facility.

Alternate Growth Patterns

On the other side, there are those who contend that the city is an anachronism and we should now be looking for new ways of living and working. Proponents of this view point out that the city was born of the need for man to congregate near the waterways so he could transport both goods and people. And the railroads connected these already-existing cities, and so, they, too, followed pre-fixed routes. But roads and the motor vehicle—the automobile and the truck—have removed the need for man to congregate at any one specific place, or to follow any one specific route, and have, in fact, freed him to locate virtually anyplace.

Yet man is not locating just anyplace, as we already have seen. He is locating, for the most part, in the suburbs, which have experienced a population increase of 28 percent since 1960, as compared to only a 1 percent increase for all central cities.

"This trend continues in part because of the strong economic and cultural attractions of the large metropolitan areas—including Government policies and program expenditures—that tend to reinforce existing concentrations of population and economic activity."

So reads the report of the National Goals Research Staff, which continues: "Hence, the choice of no change in public policy, as discussed earlier in this chapter, would run the high risk of bringing about the kind of future in which the communities of both urban and rural America would further deteriorate. It means that hundreds of American towns will continue to lose young people and economic opportunity; and that the large metropolitan areas, already burdened with social and fiscal problems and characterized by fragmentation of governmental responsibility, may reach a size at which they will be socially intolerable, politically unmanageable, and economically inefficient.

"On the other hand, there is the choice of decisive public policy and action to achieve a different and more promising future for the country as a whole. The objective of this choice might be to promote more balanced demographic growth in order to affect the quality of life in both urban and rural America."

The report goes on to say that it might be a good idea to attract people away from the urban complexes: "Apropos of population distribution, we need to decide on whether or not we will adopt a deliberate strategy to encourage internal migration to negate the forecasts of ever-growing congestion in a few megalopoli. A viable option for such an alternative strategy is a policy of encouraging growth in alternate growth centers away from the large urban masses, coupled with a complementary effort on the use of new towns."

In the halls of Congress, in the White House, in State houses, and in the business community, there is a great deal of activity concerning the concept of new communities. And certainly such a concentration of attention would seem to forecast a growing involvement in this area. In other words, Federal, State and local governments may be expected to give an increasing impetus to the building of communities away from urban centers.

This challenge is really not the role of government. Nor should it be. It may not even be possible, in a free society, to expect that. It is a challenge to government, industry, and people jointly.

Such governmental activity will encourage the assistance of the private sector to supply the housing, industry, jobs and other needs and wants of people who will make up these communities removed from urban centers.

However, government, official spokesman for the people, may have to take the lead.

On the Federal level, where major impetus is expected to be given to the trend, rivalries already have sprung up among various departments over the authority for doling out Federal assistance for the building of new communities. The Department of Housing and Urban Development has been administering a program for new communities under Title IV of the HUD Act of 1968, but this has been a rather contained program and HUD Secretary Romney has since recommended a much more ambitious undertaking, one that calls for an initial outlay of $220 million to help stimulate the development of 10 new communities a year over a five-year period. As of this writing, the proposal was on the shelf, put aside temporarily by President Nixon because of inflation.

A number of Senators and Congressmen have voiced more than passing interest in the subject, with Rep. Thomas L. Ashley, D-Ohio, coming forth with the biggest plan, a community development bill that could cost, according to HUD officials, as much as $22 billion over five years.

In introducing the bill to the House of Representatives in March, 1970, Representative Ashley had this to say:

"Mr. Speaker, we have had a half-century of rapid urbanization in the United States during which the Federal Government has taken a 'watch-Topsy-grow' attitude. The time has come to start shaping events in our urban society rather than have events shape us. Demands for a decent living environment can only be satisfied if we have a national policy to use all our resources for rational urban development—both physical and socioeconomic."

Certainly, this action and interest in the concept of new towns as one answer to the problem of urban stagnation are in themselves highly indicative of what the future holds.

New towns are springing up all over—near Houston, Tex.; Baltimore, Fort Lauderdale, Sacramento, New Orleans, and elsewhere. It is estimated that more than 100 new communities are in the building or planning stage. Strictly speaking, most of them are not new towns. A "new town" is supposed to be self-sustaining and not within the sphere of influence of an established city. This is the definition accepted by most authorities, but most of the so-called new towns being built are really satellite towns—apart from, but dependent to some extent on, the central mother city.

But whether a new community is within commuting distance of a major city and under its influence or whether it is far removed from any such influence— as is Lake Havasu City, Ariz., which is being built on the other side of a 45-mile lake from the Southern California megalopolis—the residents will be dependent —perhaps exclusively—on the motor vehicle for personal transportation as well as the delivery of goods and products.

Rural development is another imaginative concept for relieving urban congestion that is attracting wide attention.

"The great threat that now faces us is that the social and economic ills of the Nation's inner cities may worsen and spread over entire urban areas, infecting even the entire national structure unless we act together with intelligence to prevent it. . . . Yet, the answer to the problem of rural migration and the solution to the central city plagues are as close by as America's countryside."

So reads "A New Life for the Country—The Report of the President's Task Force on Rural Development."

This task force, headed by Mrs. Haven Smith, National Chairman of the American Farm Bureau Women, and including recognized authorities from the academic and business worlds, calls for an extensive program to reverse the march of the populace from the country to the city. Tax incentives for companies locating in rural sections and a Rural Development Credit Bank to provide loans for improving housing, sewage, electric power, recreational facilities and for other programs are among the task force recommendations.

Still another approach to relieving metropolitan congestion is one calling for the encouragement of growth in middle-sized and small communities.

Accelerated growth appears to be taking place among the second-level cities, while indications are that the largest metropolitan areas are experiencing a slowing in their growth. Projected population growth tables from 1965 to 1975 issued by the Bureau of the Census show that the giant metropolitan centers will experience considerably less growth in those years than the national average. Growth rates for the period were projected to be highest for metropolitan areas of 1 million to 2 million inhabitants and lowest for areas with more than 2 million. Thus, such areas as Atlanta, Houston, Dallas, Denver, San Jose and Sacramento all are growing more rapidly than Chicago, New York, Detroit and Philadelphia.

"The obvious conclusion," says a Census Bureau official, "is that the giant cities are getting too big and are becoming inefficient. All the problems—moving people around, smog, sewage—are getting worse. These cities are experiencing what Chinitz calls the diseconomics of scale, and growth is slowing as a result."

However, this development does not promise relief for our congested areas. Quite the contrary. The second-level cities that are experiencing considerable growth all lie within the 12 great metropolitan areas mentioned previously.

Relief could come, in part, from stimulating growth in the smaller cities and towns. And such growth—all surveys seem to agree—is and will be dependent on modern, efficient highways. Take Hazard, Kentucky, an example cited by a report from the Federal Highway Administration published in June, 1970. New highways recently reduced travel time from Hazard to Lexington from 3½ to 1½ hours. "Hazard is a mountain community with excess workers who can now commute to Lexington where jobs are available," the report reads.

Jobs for Hazard residents, quite naturally, pump new blood into the Hazard economy.

The report cites other examples, including those areas lying near the Connecticut Turnpike. "The Connecticut Turnpike was built primarily to improve the local economy, not to meet existing traffic demands," the report reads. "The benefits expected have materialized. Manufacturing employment in the area served by the Turnpike increased by 27 percent between 1956 and 1962, compared to no change for the State as a whole and to a slight decline in the control areas some distance from the Turnpike."

None of these approaches for sound population dispersal—new communities, rural development and development of the smaller cities and towns—has been implemented on a scale that will have a noticeable effect in the foreseeable future. And none is a panacea in itself. But all three offer great hope as alternative growth patterns—provided sufficient stimulus is forthcoming. The Federal government, along with State and local governments, with the assistance of business and industry, can bring about these changes. And because of the high mobility of the motor vehicle, the field of transportation and marketing has the capability of responding to such alternate growth patterns with facility and efficiency.

Affluence and Discretionary Income

Perhaps one of the strangest commentaries on American life today is the oft-heard complaint—which is at the same time a compliment—about the abundance of products. "There are too many products," housewives across the land are heard to say. "It's too hard to choose."

It is a complaint that pays tribute, admittedly in a backhanded way, to technology, transportation and marketing. The housewife of fifty years ago could not have voiced such a complaint and would have had a hard time understanding it. And you don't have to go back that far. Just 20 years ago the average supermarket carried only 1,500 items; today that supermarket carries 8,000 items.

There is no indication that this prolificacy will cease, although consumer reaction may result in better and more complete product information, and the introduction of "new" products, which are insignificantly different from products already being marketed by the same manufacturer may be curtailed. But this would not, presumably, affect the total amount of goods and products being sold, only the labeling and quality.

The prolificacy of goods that is a sign of our times is not just in the form of a multiplicity of choice of breakfast foods or automobiles, but also is reflected in the choice of a multitude of products and services available. These choices are available only because enough consumers have enough spending money to buy things over and above what they actually need. This discretionary spending is a vital force in our overall economy. In the Depression year of 1936, only 20 percent of total monies spent came under the heading of "discretionary spending." Today Americans are spending $175 billion a year—fully half their total income —on nonessentials, and by 1980, it is predicted, this discretionary spending will skyrocket to 80 percent of the total.

Also consider, that even for "essentials," the average man is spending more for better quality than ever before. Not long ago there was a great deal of difference in the tables set before the wealthy man in his mansion and the one set before the average breadwinner in his modest dwelling. Today, the shop apprentice is on just as good terms with a T-bone as the chairman of the board.

Barring disaster, the average American consumer will continue to have more and more money to spend on non-essentials, such as boats, travel, entertainment, camping and recreational equipment, a second or even a third car, flight lessons and perhaps an airplane, and so on, and more time to enjoy it all, thanks to shorter work weeks—in the future.

In other words, the kinds and amount of such products and services available will expand with the demand, with absolutely no reduction in the demand for and availability of the essentials. People will eat just as much and as well, if not better, but they'll have more money and more time for other things. All of this expanding demand will, of course, mean additional requirements from our transportation and marketing facilities. All the additional products that will be in demand as a result of this increased discretionary income will have to be carried from point of production to point of final purchase by consumer, and projections clearly show a marked increase in transportation facilities in the years ahead.

Affluence and the Rise of Minorities

As the population increases, as the standard of living rises, as discretionary income grows, more specialized markets appear on the scene. For the major characteristic of discretionary income is that it is discretionary, thus allowing the individual to spend it according to his own desires. Boating and camping are examples. Whole industries have grown up over these pursuits. Moreover, a glance at a magazine rack in virtually any drugstore will point up the extent of these specialized interests. In fact, the magazine field itself has shown a marked swing away from general interest publications to special interest magazines.

The general affluence with its discretionary incomes also has drawn lines around larger "special interest" groups—primarily youth, women, and the minorities, especially Negroes. Youth, of course, spends a lot of money on non-essentials. "The way they turn an item into a fad one day, then drop it the next, can be the bane of long-range planners but a boon to marketers who learn how to spot trends fast, field a product quickly and drop it pronto if it proves to have a short market life," says Business Management Magazine.

More and more, women have been coming into their own as wage-earners and free spenders. They may be expected to have more discretionary income at their disposal as their drive for equality on the job continues to make headway.

The working woman is not an insignificant force. She numbers 30 million. Most working women—78 percent—are or have been married. Where two separate wage earners are bringing paychecks into the same household—and this is increasingly the case, particularly in the younger age groups—the result is a significant increase in discretionary spending power.

As for the black community, which spends about $40 billion a year, the question still to be decided, some contend, is whether it should be treated as a separate market or as part of the overall market. For example, magazines directed at Negroes have been on the market for years, and recently a greeting-card company has been putting out cards especially for Negroes. On the other hand, such specialization would be limited and for most marketing purposes Negroes will be considered, along with whites, as plain potential consumers.

Contributing to a growing economy is the emerging spending power of Negroes and other minority groups. Negroes, in particular, have been experiencing a marked climb on the economic scale. In the 1960s, the Census Bureau reports, Negro families living in poverty dropped from 48 percent to 29 percent. In 1970, 56 percent of Negroes were earning a minimum of $5,000 annually, as compared to 37 percent 10 years ago. In the $10,000-plus bracket, the 10-year improvement for Negroes has been from 8 percent to 21 percent.

Negroes still lag behind whites, but they are closing the gap. The average family income for Negroes is 63 percent of the average for whites, but 10 years ago it was only 55 percent of the figure for white families.

While statistics are not often exhilarating, these are most impressive because they show conclusively that poverty need not be a way of life for anybody in the United States.

Other minority groups also can look forward to better days. In July of 1970, during hearings before the Subcommittee on Migratory Labor of the Senate Committee on Labor and Public Welfare, testimony from officials of business corporations and farm cooperatives clearly showed a growing concern for and marked improvement in the conditions of the migrant worker.

Rural development projects, previously discussed, are raising and will continue to raise the standard of living of families in the areas affected.

In short, the lot of all minorities will undoubtedly improve in an expanding economy and in an atmosphere of cooperation and good will, so that the time may not be far off when the word "minority" will apply only to population reports.

People:
How They Work

All wage earners—black, white, male and female—
make up the labor market, that mammoth, sprawling,
complex entity whose changing nature is of supreme
importance in any attempt to understand the changes
in the social structure as a whole.

We already have examined the shift in the labor force from a predominantly
agri-mining force to an industrial force—and even while that transformation continues, still another transpires. But now the shift is from the production of goods
to the production of services, and it is occurring for the very same reason the
shift from farm to industry has been happening—greater productivity.

Moreover, the entire labor force is in the midst of great growth. That baby
crop of the post World War II era is moving into the labor market. An estimated
18.5 million new workers are expected to be added to that force during this
decade. And youth—with its vigor, imagination and eagerness for change—will
make up a greater proportion of the entire labor force than ever before.

It is, of course, the labor force which produces the total output of goods and
services known as the GNP (Gross National Product). And conversely, a growing
GNP in a sense creates more and more jobs. The GNP rose from a shade over
$500 billion in 1960 to $932 billion in 1969, creating 12 million new jobs. By 1980,
the GNP is expected to soar to nearly $2 trillion, and—even allowing for price
inflation—this expansion will call for an increase in the labor force from a 1969
figure of about 84 million to more than 100 million.

These additional wage earners—many of whom will be starting their own
households—will, in themselves, be consumers and will be putting additional
demands on transportation and marketing.

Of particular importance is that shift of the labor market away from the
production of goods to the production of services, a shift that has been gaining
momentum as an ever-advancing technology (in manufacturing plant as well as
on farm) improves the productivity. Shortly after the turn of the century, the
Bureau of Labor Statistics tells us, only 3 in every 10 workers were in service
industries. By 1950, a little more than 5 in every 10 were in service industries. In
1968, the figure had jumped to 6 in 10; by 1980, close to 7 of every 10 workers will
be in service industries—68 million out of 100 million.

The service industries are, of course, that growing multitude of non-goods
producers and include transportation, communications, public utilities, wholesale

and retail trades, household, health, educational and business services, and government.

The Bureau of Labor Statistics expects an upswing in employment in the transportation field, which in the postwar years has been dominated by the decline in railroad employment. Says a BLS report, "The U.S. Economy in 1980," published in 1970: "But a turn around is expected: trucking and air transportation will increase fast enough to offset whatever further small railroad declines occur; an overall slow gain in employment is expected."

All modes are expected to show significant increases in the transportation of goods. Total revenues of regulated interstate carriers are expected to climb from $22.4 billion in 1967 to $38.4 billion in 1980. Ton-miles (a ton of freight carried one mile) will go up from a 1967 total of 1.8 billion to a 1980 figure of 3 billion.

More transportation facilities will be needed because there will be more goods to be hauled to more people, despite the shift of employment to the service industries. Motor truck registrations, which now number 17 million, are expected to soar to 25 million by 1980. Among the goods producers, manufacturing will continue to show a rise in number of employees. This, the largest single source of jobs in the economy, employed 20 million persons in 1968 and will employ 22.4 million in 1980.

Agriculture, along with forestries and fisheries, will continue to show a decline, while construction will show an increase of 1½ million employees between now and 1980.

As may be expected from a nation of high productivity and relative affluence, the big rise in the production of durable goods will be in such non-essentials as television sets, records, musical instruments, and sporting and recreational goods. "Americans will have more time on their hands and money to spend than ever before," predicts the National Planning Association, "and the leisure industry will be the principal beneficiary of this rising affluence. The surge to the outdoors and the upsurge in the number of Americans who ski, play golf and tennis will mean a sharply rising demand for sporting goods, pleasure boats and other related equipment."

For every 100 workers in 1980, 32 will be producing goods and 68 will be in the service industries. Of the 32 goods producers, only 3 will be in agriculture (compared to the 99 out of every 100 tilling the soil in the Middle Ages); 6 in construction, 1 in mining, and 22 in manufacturing. Of the 68 workers in the non-goods industries, 21 will be in the heterogeneous group that includes personal, business, health, and educational services; 20 will be in the wholesale and retail trades (including general merchandising stores and eating and drinking establishments); 5 will be in transportation, communications and public utilities; 5 more will be in finance, insurance, and real estate, and 17 will be in government.

This labor force in years and decades ahead will be better educated, with 7 million more college graduates to be added by 1980. A better educated labor force will be much better able to deal with the growing complexities of our society, and it may also be expected to be more demanding of society, including itself. In the light of today's emphasis among the young on bettering the conditions of all Americans, tomorrow's labor force might well speed up the programs now under way to achieve that noteworthy goal.

Changes Are Taking Place

Even as this is being read, changes are taking place in that fascinating, all-encompassing world of technology. Schlesinger's "increase in the velocity of history" continues apace, so much so that the futuristic comic strips so popular a generation ago couldn't keep up today—a startling new breakthrough by Buck Rogers or Flash Gordon could in reality become obsolete while the strip was running through the presses.

This fact of life is graphically illustrated in the report by the National Goals Research Staff which notes that the span of change for photography (from time of conception to time of sociological impact) was 112 years, while for the transistor it was just 3 years, and for the solar battery, 2 years.

"Each of these items has had profound social consequences and most of them will continue to have such consequences for years to come," reads the National Goals Research Staff report. "Each example may be characterized as describing a cluster of many discreet scientific and technological developments that together have resulted in new social trends. The impact of the data is that with increasing rapidity knowledge is converted into useful products which produce social change. Hence, the problem of anticipating social change becomes increasingly formidable."

Still, one may safely predict continuing improvement in communications. Picture phones, portable individual telephones, and computers for the home are among reasonable things to expect.

Better ways to predict the weather and even means for controlling it may be over the horizon. Certainly, man will continue in his exploration of space and depth, with the oceans holding promise of a greater food supply and perhaps a good answer to the waste disposal problem.

In the field of health, we can look forward to that long-awaited life-prolonging breakthrough in the battles against cancer and cardiovascular ailments, while organ transplants may become as commonplace as extractive surgery is today. Surely whole new generations of sophisticated pharmaceutical products will be discovered, researched, proved, and marketed.

Transportation and marketing, of course, will be affected by all of this. Healthier, longer-living people mean more production and more consumption. Farming the oceans will call for additional transportation facilities of an intermodal nature to carry the products from sea to dining table.

And most assuredly, transportation and marketing—like all other areas of man's society—will in themselves experience greater efficiencies due to the march of technology. Like other service industries—including law, education, medicine, business, and government—transportation is expected to receive a tremendous boost from the computer. Transportation systems of the future will be relying more and more on electronics to improve their service and efficiency. Computers, which up to now have been used for the most part for the maintaining of records, are expected to play prominent roles in facilitating the loading and unloading of vehicles, the routing and re-routing of vehicles, the transferring and storing of products, general communications and other areas.

Other devices and techniques for future transportation and marketing are not in focus, but may well include new kinds of vehicles and new kinds of power sources, perhaps nuclear or solar, or even some power not imagined today.

The challenge to today's marketing men—those specialists who mastermind the movement of people's needs and wants—is to read the signs that signal changes to come; to interpret influences; to counsel management and government; to keep a step ahead of demand. And indeed, the times that face today's marketing men are most challenging—perhaps more so than ever before in all our creative and inventive periods of progress and achievement.

Conclusion

Life—it was pointed out in the beginning of this chapter—is in a whirl. But it need not be a self-defeating whirl. Compared to any other time in history, there is more right with today's world than wrong.

And in making this better life, man also has introduced some unforeseen and undesirable elements. Chapter One explored those elements that were ecological in nature—the fouling of air, land, and water—and attempted to relate them and possible solutions to transportation and marketing. In this chapter, we have examined the elements that are more sociological in nature—population congestion, a changing labor market, the emergence of minority groups, advancing technology, etc. Our purpose has not been to come up with solid answers, for such a purpose would be arrogant and impractical, but rather to stimulate those among us who are involved or interested in marketing and transportation now and in the future.

In both Chapters, our attitude of optimism has been deliberate. In our view, these ecological and sociological elements are not so much problems as they are challenges that must be met by all the people—manufacturer and producer, transportation and marketing people, government, business, and industry and housewife. For these challenges are the effects of the sum total of the living done by all of us.

As such, these challenges, both ecological and sociological, are the by-products of an affluent age. The eager idealist—so right in his concern for the less fortunate—often overlooks the fact that the less fortunate do not exist, or, at least, are not recognized, in a society where virtually everybody is unfortunate. It is only an affluent people who can afford to be concerned about sociological challenges. Viewed in that light, the concern so evident in America today—for the poor, the uneducated, the less privileged—is a tribute to, not an indictment of, the free enterprise system.

The free enterprise system in the United States has given us a standard of living unprecedented and undreamed of a short while ago. And certainly there is a solid basis for believing that the complete elimination of poverty and the successful solution of all the other matters about where and how man will live are realistic goals—exciting challenges.

"But roads and the motor vehicle have removed the need for man to congregate at any one specific place . . ."

Satellite cities (bottom): "New towns are springing up all over . . ."

*The new town
of Reston, Virginia—
man's answer
to urban sprawl?*

Photo by Blue Ridge Aerial Survey

3

Transportation
and the
Technological
Revolution

Chapter Three

Transportation
and the
Technological
Revolution

Prologue
to Tomorrow

Five or six thousand years ago—give or take a month—the Thomas Edison of his day invented the wheel.

That wheel is still turning.

It has carried men ever upward. It has led from crude wagons to powered chariots . . . from back-breaking labor to control of an army of efficient machines . . . from earth to moon.

But it took man five or six thousands years to progress from the invention of the wheel to the invention of the automobile.

And then came the deluge!

What has been happening in very recent years, and what is happening today, seem more like science-fiction than reality. And what is happening today, we can be assured, is a prologue to what will come tomorrow.

The Industrial Revolution that started in the 18th century eventually changed man and his working habits drastically and dramatically. The harnessing of the first steam engine to the first loom spelled the end of man's role as a beast-of-burden with a brain. In time, he no longer would be required to spend virtually all of his working hours doing the things necessary to stay alive. He would still have to work, but now great machinery was there to aid him and give him more free time than he had ever had before, including free time to think, to philosophize, and to make even better and more efficient machines to do his bidding.

Now we are in the midst of another great revolution—an extension of the Industrial Revolution, but so overwhelming in its own right that it must be regarded as a separate life force, even perhaps, a brand new creation. If it can be left unchecked—by man-made or natural holocaust—it promises to shatter all that has gone before and raise mankind to a truly Golden Age.

This revolution is basically one of technology, but in its torrent, flood waters are spilling over into the social world. A relatively newfound freedom from the soil has sent man scurrying, in ever-increasing numbers, to live in urban complexes and to work in industry and laboratory. The marvels of electronics have given even to the humblest of men a window on the world, creating within him new needs and new desires. There has been a flow of goods from drawing board to factory to household, so that today American man has an abundance, qualitative and quantitative, unmatched anywhere, anytime in history.

And there is no denying the vital role of transportation and marketing in this drama of dramas. Without that wheel, man would still be living an isolated, primitive existence, with his road from cradle to grave paved with the cruel hardships of a life completely dedicated to survival. Indeed, transportation has literally and figuratively carried man from one age to another.

But if man now is entering a golden age, he also is being dogged by shadows. Social change has meant and continues to mean unprecedented social challenges. We have explored these social changes, including the ever-increasing crowding of man's urban complexes, the shift in the labor market from farm to factory to service industries, the growing affluence, the deluge of products, and other factors, and attempted to relate them to the world of transportation and marketing. And we also have investigated the environmental problems facing man and how they relate to transportation and marketing.

But sociological and ecological crises—as threatening as they may be—are nothing more than the fallout from the main force, which is a technological revolution. British Editor Charles Singer defines technologies as bodies of skills, knowledge and procedures for making, using and doing useful things. Technology is not science, but the application of science. And while science has been acquiring more knowledge in recent times than ever before—it is estimated that between 80 and 90 percent of all scientists who ever lived are alive today—industry has been applying that knowledge in the manufacture and marketing of products and services with unprecedented swiftness.

The French editor and social critic, J. J. Servan-Schreiber, points out that it took 112 years for photography to make its way from a mere invention to a manufactured product, 56 years for the telephone, 35 years for the radio, 15 years for radar, 12 years for television, six years for the atomic bomb.

This "increase in the velocity of history," as Arthur M. Schlesinger, Jr., calls it, is pelting man with such sudden change that, in the opinion of some observers, it is a threat to his mental stability. "We can never be really prepared for that which is wholly new," says Philosopher Eric Hoffer. "We have to adjust ourselves, and every radical adjustment is a crisis in self-esteem. . . . It needs inordinate self-confidence to face drastic change without inner trembling."

If, as one writer phrased it, the invention of the steam engine was like "the explosion of a volcano to the slowly moving agrarian society of its time," then today's technological revolution is like the birth of a solar system.

Where will it lead? And, in particular, how is it affecting and how will it affect transportation and marketing?

"To discuss the future of technology may not be the most arrogant act imaginable," says Henry M. Boettinger, Director of Management Sciences at American Telephone & Telegraph Co., "but it comes high on the list."

But let us be arrogant enough to make one prediction: Science and its offspring, Technology, will not be denied. Both are under threat today. They are being charged by some as the villains who are solely responsible for the social and ecological ills that face us. "The height of the new folly," Science Writer Lawrence Lessing says in Fortune Magazine, "is the rising call upon scientists and technicians to foresee all the consequences of their actions and to make a moral commitment to suppress work on any discovery that might some day be dangerous, which is to demand that they be not only scientists but certified clairvoyants and saints."

Lessing quotes Konrad Lorenz, the famous naturalist, who warns the hostiles among the students that their anti-science attacks could take us back 200,000 years. "Watch out!" Lorenz tells them. "If you make a clean sweep of things, you won't go back to the Stone Age, because you're already there, but to well before the Stone Age."

It is not likely to happen, however, because the acquisition of knowledge, the exploration of the unknown, the adaptation of discovery to practical living—all are as natural to man as eating, breathing and rearing families.

No one really can predict the future with any reasonable assurance of accuracy, but we can take a look—and it need not be an economic appraisal—at the major trends in the world of technological advancement today and report the routes the experts say they probably will follow. We cannot, in a study such as this, touch all the bases, nor even pause long at any one. But we can attempt to provide a newer roadmap to give those of you who are involved in the vital fields of transportation and marketing new clues as to where you are and where you may well be going.

Man on the Moon: Spinoff Benefits

"The space program is the cutting edge for science and technology," says Dr. Wernher von Braun. "Man needs a cutting edge as he hunts for truth."

We have put a man on the moon, a feat that is symbolic of our space program, but the achievement is far more than a symbol. The space program is a fit launching pad for an essay on technology, for it has been the major catalyst for the technological revolution. And while the conquest of space has been the immediate objective, the improvement of life on earth has been the immediate result.

The spinoff benefits from the space program to date have been so vast as to defy much more than a cursory glance here. But even a cursory glance will provide sufficient evidence that we are, indeed, in the midst of some exciting scientific breakthroughs. Let us keep in mind, too, that this is only the beginning. "Substantial as it is," says the "Air Force Space Digest," "the current flow from the wellspring of space technology is only a trickle compared with the flood to come. . . ."

The field of medicine has been a prime recipient of spinoff from space technology:

• New techniques in monitoring and evaluating such physical variables as the electroencephalogram (EEG), the electrocardiogram (EKG), respiratory functions, blood pressure, etc.

• A cradle warmer system that monitors the condition of prematurely born infants while maintaining the proper temperature within the laminated plastic bassinet. A direct spinoff from the "glass sandwich" used to prevent windshield fogging on the X-15 and other high altitude experimental aircraft.

• A new technology that enables technicians to transmit electrocardiograms while en route in ambulance to the hospital. It makes use of a spray-on electrode applicator used for pilot instrumentation.

• Multiple electrodes mounted in inflatable vests for exceptionally rapid EKG measurements.

• An automatic air volume monitor for the diagnosis of emphysema.

• An infra-red radiation device for measuring blood oxygen content in leukemia patients.

• A pacemaker electrode—still in the development stage—that will be inserted by a hypodermic needle rather than major surgery.

• A device for precise fitting of artificial limbs adapted from the devices used to measure the land impact of the Apollo Command module.

• A new technique for the treatment of the handicapped and the rehabilitation of patients who have difficulty walking again after being bedridden. Adapted from a sling support device designed to familiarize astronauts with characteristics of reduced gravity on the moon.

• A cardiotachometer for accurate measurement of fetal heart rates.

• A device for measuring pressure in the heart, to be inserted by a standard hypodermic needle. It was adapted from a device that measures pressure distribution over the surface of miniature models in wind tunnels.

That is a small sampling of space spinoffs in the field of medicine alone. Other fields are benefitting also. An oil drilling firm is now using an accelerometer developed for use on space launching towers. A device used for damping vibration of engine compressor blades in the space program is now being adapted to overcome gear train vibration problems in the manufacture of clutches for heavy duty trucks. A new plastic called hystyl, a thermo-setting urethane plastic, can be processed but remains very stable at high temperatures.

Everyone is familiar with the meteorological satellites, which have vastly improved weather forecasting, but few realize the number of lives saved by this system. Hurricane Camille, which roared across Louisiana and Mississippi in August, 1969, killed 258 persons, while another 68 were reported missing. But without the early warnings, made possible by the meteorological satellites, government officials estimate the toll might have gone as high as 50,000.

Fairly well known, too, is the contribution of space research and development to the field of communications. Communications satellites have made global television a reality and trans-Atlantic telephone service commonplace. One satellite provides about ten times the channel capacity of an underwater cable.

The space program never could have gotten off the ground without the computer. Before each launching, hundreds of programs involving hundreds of thousands of steps must be fed into the electronic machines. But the benefits have been reciprocal, as the space program has served as a catalyst for the computer revolution. Today the National Aeronautics and Space Administration has a softwear inventory of almost 1,000 programs that can be converted to business use. A businessman can get a computer program for from one-half to one-tenth what it would cost him to develop a similar program from scratch.

The NASA/RECON (remote console) service gives users thousands of miles apart almost instant machine access to the central information store. Seated at a console with a cathode-ray tube and typewriter keyboard, each user of RECON can ask the computer in Maryland what documents have been deposited in the NASA storehouse that meet his particular needs. A quick response will show up on the cathode ray. If he wants detailed information, he can order the computer to mail it to him, or to print it out on a printer beside the cathode-ray tube.

In the field of management, NASA has picked up valuable experience and is making it available for the asking. The House Committee on Science and Astronautics in a recent report termed the overall organizational program behind the Apollo flights "extraordinary." To make the space program work, the report declared, it was "necessary to marshal the resources of some 20,000 contractors, to coordinate their work, to insure an orderly flow of components to the assembly lines, to build new facilities, to maintain equipment quality and reliability, to perform a thousand other tasks."

The orderly, efficient transportation of material and supplies to the building and launching sites, which contributed to the efficiency of the overall program, is a credit to the transportation industry.

The city of Los Angeles, for one, has taken advantage of the availability of the NASA management and communications techniques to plan a command and control system that would "provide rapid pinpointing of field forces, computer dispatching, automated status displays, computerized information fields, individual communications for hazardous-duty personnel, and automatic transmission and signalling for emergency vehicles."

The list of spinoff benefits from space is almost endless. Research is now going on to utilize the deceleration force techniques of our space ships to minimize injury in automobile accidents. Automated surface traffic control and sensors to prevent train derailment, along with noise reduction techniques, and new methods of refuse disposal and water reclamation are under development.

One of the more intriguing results of our man-on-the-moon program and one that was totally unexpected involved an experiment with the moon soil brought back by the crew of Apollo 11. A moss-like plant called liverwort was planted in earth soil and moon soil at the Houston Manned Space Flight Center. Neither soil was fertilized. The plants in the lunar soil grew significantly faster and reached greater size than the plants in the earth soil, prompting the late Rep. James G. Fulton of Pennsylvania to remark: "To me this has great significance. If we are able to determine what caused the lunar plants to grow faster and larger than the others, think what this will mean to the food problems plaguing the world. Think what this would mean in terms of manpower that could be released from agriculture in the underdeveloped nations out to an expanding industrial base necessary for economic development."

In referring to spinoff benefits from space, Congressman Fulton brought us back to earth. And this is the point that is missed by those who would place space programs on the opposite end of the scale from earth programs, such as the war on poverty, and insist that one is in direct opposition to the other. If a space program can teach man to grow better crops with greater yield, then it is an important combatant in the war against poverty.

Let us keep in mind, too, that a space program is possible only where enough of the components—men, knowledge and materials—are available. And this availability is a by-product of high efficiency in those areas dealing with basic necessities, such as the production of food, clothing and shelter. If it took virtually all of us—as it once did—scratching the soil from dawn to dusk to provide the needed food crops, there would be nobody left over to send to the moon. These spinoff benefits from space have a great more value than is readily discernible.

Most significant and highly promising is the fact that this magnificent beneficence scores high in both quality and quantity, assuring—if left unchecked—an ever-increasing higher standard of living. This, in turn, even without a population increase, would necessitate greater dependence on transportation and marketing—the twin supports for any civilized foundation, while transportation and marketing, themselves, also would share in the bounty from space, as their operations (be it diminished clutch vibrations or a better refrigerated body) became more efficient and more economical.

It is estimated that the entire store of information in the world's libraries amounts to 10^{15} (one quadrillion, or one million billion) bits. This information is stored in the form of books and other printed documents, and is doubling every 15 to 20 years. A leading computer manufacturer has recently announced the commercial availability of a new type of direct-access computer memory that will hold 10^{12} bits (a thousand billion), or one-thousandth of the world's recorded information. There appears the possibility that by 1980 a small number of computers will replace all the written documentation existing in the world, and that they will work in "real time"—replying to questions with information at the speed of human conversation.

—J. J. Servan-Schreiber
 "The American Challenge"

All the Answers

No essay on technological advances can move very far without entering the world of the computer. The computer is the basis for the revolution, which is a revolution that feeds on information. In 1955, there were only 1,000 computers in the United States; today there are 70,000—and they are growing in number, diminishing in size and increasing in capacity and versatility. Japan ranks No. 2 with only 5,800 computers, while the Soviet Union is sixth with 3,500.

In 1965, when there were only 20,000 computers in the United States, Jerry Carlson wrote in Farm Management Magazine: "At least a dozen of the 20,000 computers in the United States have touched your life since you woke up this morning. They're processing your checks, keeping your credit card accounts, figuring the averages you hear on the market news, blending your livestock concentrates, helping predict tomorrow's weather and formulating your breakfast sausage. All this in ten short years since the computer age began."

Transportation
and the
Technological
Revolution

In 1966, David Sarnoff, Chairman of the Board of Radio Corporation of America, said in an issue of Saturday Review: "In just ten years, the typical electronic data processor has become ten times smaller, 100 times faster, and 1,000 times less expensive to operate."

And the trend toward more, faster, smaller, less expensive and more efficient continues.

In today's technological world—and even more so in tomorrow's—quick access to tons of information is vital. "Consider my own case as an example," says Alec H. Reeves of International Telephone & Telegraph, inventor of the Pulse Code Modulation. "It would take me even now about 30 hours in each day of a seven-day week to keep thoroughly up to date in all the scientific and technological subjects that I really need to know in my own sphere of circuitry research alone, if I were to digest and consider properly all that I read. By A.D. 2000, it would be even more impossible."

(Pulse Code Modulation, incidentally, is a new technology in digital transmission that breaks down all messages—verbal and printed—into electronic signals that travel at the rate of 8,000 pulses a second. However, this study will not attempt to delve into actual workings of the electronic marvels on the market and drawing boards. In fact, most of those who will be making use of these technological wonders won't understand them, nor will it be necessary. It is not necessary to hold a degree in veterinary medicine in order to ride a horse.)

And the downpour continues. While one just begins to assimilate the latest breakthroughs in computers and communications already in operation, more exotic ones appear on the horizon. For example, laboratories now are working on a new kind of computer, where electronic impulses will travel not along wires— but along beams of light, laser beams! The result will be not a million processing steps per second, but a billion!

So fast does the downpour of technological wonder descend that one can't keep up. Today's realities seem like tomorrow's dreams:

• From a cavernous reservation center in a large Southern city, agents, working at 150 consoles, keep track of more than 2 million air lines reservations simultaneously.

• At 11:56 a.m., Eastern Standard Time, on a Friday in April, a computer in the Federal Bureau of Investigation's National Crime Information Center in Washington receives a message about a man arrested in Denver. Within seconds, the computer acknowledges and flashes back the message that the man also is wanted in Oklahoma City for armed robbery.

• In McComb, Mississippi, a computer assigns work to a 6-year-old student, grades her work, and, when the class is over, prints a cheery "Goodbye, Sheila."

• In a Midwest bakery, a computer gathers up and mixes the proper ingredients, reads 300 different temperatures every 20 seconds, oversees the running of a football-field-sized warehouse, and turns out 800 cakes a minute.

• In Pittsburgh, a computer programs the proper mixing of ingredients for iron in a blast furnace and controls the rolling of steel slabs into sheets thin enough to sheathe cars, trucks and refrigerators.

• In Washington, D.C., at the site of a complex of modern, round, walled-in-glass apartment buildings, a project manager takes his hard hat off in a reverential gesture as he talks about a computer: "Each concrete floor reaches out to a slightly different edge. Those glass walls are really hundreds of separate windows, set in hundreds of steel frames, each of slightly different breadth! To get the necessary specifications takes hundreds of thousands of calculations. Even if we could get enough engineers to do it, they'd each make little errors, and the pieces wouldn't fit properly. Some computer figured it all. It sends specifications to the manufacturer for each window and frame. Each arrives labeled as to precise location."

• Deep inside the Cheyenne Mountains, near Colorado Springs, an Air Force general speaks: "The only nation in the world that can launch an all-out nuclear strike on us is the Soviet Union. And so our biggest radars look more than 3,000 miles over the horizon into the Eurasian landmass, from England, Greenland and Alaska. They pick up a rocket launch. Is it a test? Or a space shot? Or an attack on the North American Continent? Within a minute computers calculate the trajectory and display the answer. If it should be an attack, they predict the impact area. We'd get 15 to 25 minutes' warning. . . ."

• Computers match men with jobs, instantly flash results of a sale on the New York Stock Exchange to 9,000 tickers and display boards around the world, keep track of inventory for a chain of women's dress shops, and regulate traffic in a big city, adjusting signal lights to traffic flow.

• At Massachusetts Institute of Technology, a professor ridiculed the idea that a computer could think and then challenged a computer to a game of chess—and lost!

Computers in Transportation

Truck owners are becoming alarmed, noted a recent article in Transport Topics, the trucking industry's weekly newspaper, because of the bogged-down traffic in many of our cities. It has been estimated that in Washington, D.C., alone, the cost to all road users has been $69 million each year because traffic cannot move at an optimal speed of about 30 m.p.h.

Experiments have shown that computer-operated traffic signals can increase the flow of vehicles up to 50 percent, while television and underground sensory surveillance systems can spot traffic tie-ups and convey the information immediately to traffic indicators, which then re-direct vehicles away from the obstructed areas.

In Toronto, where a computer has been hooked up to what ultimately will be a 1,000 intersection system, a considerably less extensive operation has cut down traveling time by 73 percent, while motorists are enjoying 86 percent fewer involuntary stops and 12 percent fewer accidents. Certainly, the cities of the future will have electronic and computerized systems to regulate traffic flow. Shippers, businessmen and consumers will be primary beneficiaries as transportation costs are lowered, the logical result of savings in time spent by carriers en route.

The computer already has gained a strong foothold in handling, shipping, receiving and warehousing and is expected to take over more and more of these operations for all modes in the years to come.

"Data bases have been developed beyond the imagination of managers of a generation ago," states a recent article in Handling & Shipping Magazine. "Millions of bits of information can be stored on a short city block of magnetic tape, or a disc storage system not much larger than a stack of LP records. The computer can access and manipulate this total storage in seconds. The solutions to problems in turn generate additional, frequently more precise data, as well as improved techniques to aid in the solution of future problems."

Lee Way Motor Freight, Inc., of Oklahoma City has a computer system which gives immediate location of any one or all of the company's 1,325 line-haul trailers scattered over 14 states, as well as the status of each—whether it is loaded or unloaded, en route, etc.

Gordons Transports, Inc., a medium sized carrier operating out of Memphis, began using punch-card equipment 15 years ago and has progressed since to the more sophisticated equipment. "If we operated the way we did just six years ago," says John K. Gordon, Vice President-Traffic and Sales, "we'd have to have fantastic rate increases just to stay in business. The trucking business changes so fast it's all but impossible to update manually."

Since installing a complete automated system in 1968, Gordons' loss and damage claims have been cut by two-thirds. "Before the computer," says Jimmie Black, Director of Maintenance, in a recent article in Terminal Operator Magazine, "we had instances of 12 batteries being put in one tractor at six different locations. We lost between 7 and 10 percent of our speedometer cables."

The Ringsby System and United-Buckingham Freight Lines, Inc., used a computer to inventory all of its office equipment. "Now within a half an hour, the computer prints out a complete list, which includes updated information about all our office equipment," an official says. "With the information on filing cards, it would take one clerk two months to provide the same information."

Portable computers now are on the market enabling salesmen in the field to plug into a telephone and feed orders directly to a central computer, which sends out proper instructions to the warehouse and shipping personnel. Products can be en route moments after the salesman hangs up the phone. And computers can give management an instantaneous view of the kind of traffic needed at any given time to make for practical operations.

The railroads, with their far-flung operations and their thousands of units to hook up, decouple, transfer, load and unload, are utilizing automation also, as expected. Here is a description of a computerized railroad switch yard in Kansas City, from a recent edition of National Geographic:

"The tracks fan out from the hump, an incline that feeds cars onto the proper tracks for assembly into trains. Once the domain of the switchman, such yards today take orders from computers. The machine stores in its memory a list of what cars to shunt where. After yard engines have pushed cars up the far side of the hump, the computer activates the proper switches, then brakes the car for safe link-up."

A computer now gives one railroad instant information on any of its 36,000 boxcars so that empty ones can be located immediately and put to use.

Keeping track of, and getting optimum use from, box cars—that now total almost 2 million—have been a growing problem with the railroad industry as a whole, but a new system known as TRAIN (Tele Rail Automated Information Network) promises a workable solution. Utilizing a computer system and the WATS telephone lines, TRAIN already has begun operations in furnishing up-to-date data on all rolling stock to all participating roads.

Southern Pacific has installed a $22 million information system that, in the words of F. E. Kriebel, Vice President-Traffic of the line, "enables us to keep an 'astronaut's eye' on our whole 14,000-mile plant, with instantaneous information on the status of 2,200 locomotives and 91,000 freight cars.

"Such advances are taking place industry-wide. . . . In our yards at Houston, Texas, and Eugene, Oregon, computers are today making up trains, automatically weighing cars, setting the switches so they can move to their proper tracks, and automatically applying retarders so our cars glide to a gentle coupling with the train they are joining."

Merchant ship satellite communications is now a reality and so is satellite navigation that enables ships at sea and planes in the air to pinpoint their precise locations at any given time.

Some ships are equipped with automated engine room controls that make whatever adjustments are necessary to obey speed directions from the bridge.

Under development are some rather sophisticated automatic controls that will—in a few years, experts say—enable a ship to travel virtually port to port with all hands off, so to speak. Those aboard would be there to monitor the equipment and make corrections if necessary.

Ships already are equipped with collision warning devices, while some port facilities have in operation tanker loading and unloading computers. These computers load and unload tankers in such a way as not to build up undue stresses in the hull. Other computers help to load containers in a manner calculated to give the ship the greatest stability.

For aircraft, computers and computer-assisted marvels already are serving pilot and copilot, navigator and engineer, flight control operators and handling and shipping personnel.

A Day in Your Life Tomorrow

Let us now do a little projection and spell out a typical day in your life tomorrow:

You arise, bathe, shave and dress, and arrive in the kitchen just in time for breakfast, which the computer started cooking while you and your family still slept.

You push a button and the computer begins to print out the morning newspaper.

After breakfast, you decide to get on that new project of turning a basement storage room into a studio-office. You pick up your phone and tell the central computer what you plan to do. It tells you how much lumber and what kind you will need, along with how many and what kind of nails, etc.

You and your wife are entertaining tonight, so she calls another computer and tells it how many guests you will have and what she wants to serve. The computer gives her a list of supplies and tells her how much she will need of each. She tells the computer to go ahead and order the supplies and that she will want them delivered by 4 p.m.

Your wife also decides she wants a new dress for the party. She dials a department store and in a few minutes she has her own private fashion show in three dimensions on a screen in front of her. And then she stands in front of a special scanner, which takes her measurements. She asks for delivery that afternoon, and then calls the bank's computer and tells it to take care of payment.

It is a warm day and you and your family decide to go to the beach. You dial the computer and ask for the best route to take that day and almost instantly the directions are spelled out in printed form. You ease your computer car onto the automated beach highway, set the directions, and relax. Your wife tells you she forgot to turn off the television set in the game room and to lock the front door. You pick up the phone beneath the dashboard, dial your computer, and tell it to turn off the TV and lock the front door. The computer acknowledges.

You leave the automated highway, take over the controls, and hit the gas a little too heavy. A state trooper stops you and asks you to accompany him to the patrol car. He has you place your right thumb on a little screen on the dashboard. Instantly, the FBI computer in Washington puts a check through on that print and in a few minutes a voice tells the trooper who you are, that you were honorably discharged from the U.S. Marine Corps and that you have no record. The trooper lets you off with a warning.

Transportation
and the
Technological
Revolution

When you and your wife arrive back home, the party supplies and dress, ordered that morning, have been delivered by truck.

You decide to check on some office matters. You dial the office computer and ask to see some documents. You look over the documents and then ask the computer for a copy of one, and, presto, it is printed out for you on paper. You push a couple of other buttons and the images of your two partners appear on the screen. After a short conference, you dictate a letter to the computer. Your secretary will have the office computer forward that letter to the recipient's computer in the morning.

The party is a rousing success. The big hit was an information quiz game, men vs. women, in which each team asked the other difficult questions on any subject. By dialing the "all-information computer bank" the correct answers were given almost immediately. After the guests have departed, you experience pains in your stomach. They persist and you call your doctor, who tells you to hook up the computer's diagnostic sensors to the appropriate places on your body. The doctor (who has the entire sum of medical knowledge to draw on if need be) almost instantly diagnoses your trouble:

"Too much party," he says.

Sound a little far out? Well, this little fantasy is well within the realm of the expected, according to the experts, who say the basic technology for making such a day come true is already known.

In fact, you may actually be driving that computerized car by 1980, according to Douglas W. Toms, Administrator of the National Highway Traffic Safety Administration.

"I think we will have either magnetic or radio beams or metallic strips, or something that you can zero in on," Toms says, "and your solid state computer system in your car will have the ability, not only to slow it down, but to speed it up. . . . You can divert yourself from driving the car. It will just run itself."

A more immediate possibility is an electronic route guidance system for highway users. One is under testing at the Columbus (Ohio) Division of North American Rockwell, where engineers have constructed a miniature city—an exact 1/87th scale model, complete with homes, cars, trees, telephone poles, etc. A normal-sized car with no wheels, but with complete electronic route guidance equipment, "drives through" that city. The car is mounted in front of a screen, which shows a simulated drive, via closed circuit TV, through the city. The person "driving" the car actually feels that he is.

(The same kind of simulation is used by air lines to give pilots and pilot trainees the same kind of real-life experience while staying on the ground in Link trainers.)

The electronic route guidance system for highways will eliminate the need for roadside directional signs. Route directions will be flashed on a screen mounted on the car's dash. What directions will be shown will depend on the individual's destination, which he will give to his computer before starting out. Less time en route, less anxiety among drivers and improved safety are some of the benefits noted in the testing.

"There are many other benefits that could spring from such an operational system," according to Dan Rosen of the U.S. Bureau of Public Roads. "These include reduced congestion, more effective use of existing roads, increased safety, and reduced air pollution." Not to mention better looking highways, with the absence of those large, obtrusive direction signs.

Buses and trucks also will be able to use this system, and the transportation of goods by truck will be quicker and more efficient than ever.

Land, Sea and Air

Transportation—a major contributor to and beneficiary of man's progress—will be greatly affected by the new technologies.

Not only will trucks be highly automated, but they will be much more comfortable for the driver. Cabs will be temperature and humidity controlled. The trucks will be faster, more powerful and safer and will include, for example, radar-controlled anti-crash devices. Size and weight standards will reflect more realistic appraisal of highway environment, enabling trucks to carry more with greater efficiency.

Terminals will be automated and computerized to a considerable extent, so that freight may be received, sorted, loaded and delivered without being touched by human hands. And if the housewife will be able to order a dress by computer, the retailer and wholesaler, as well as the manufacturer, will be able to restock their inventories the same way.

Warehouses will be large, dust-free, quiet caverns where computers will hum out their precise instructions and humans will be on hand merely as supervisory and maintenance personnel.

Transportation
and the
Technological
Revolution

Railroads, too, can be expected to experience greater efficiencies of speed and capacities. The potential for automation in railroading has been suggested. The promise is that all railroad systems will be highly automated, with all arrivals and departures under closed circuit television surveillance, all loadings and unloadings under automatic electronic control, and product demands no longer speculative but a matter of precise forecasting.

New kinds of cars especially designed for specific purposes will make the scene. Under development is a ferry-type railroad car, which will enable passengers to drive their private autos aboard. They would park their cars on the lower deck and then depart to the upper deck to sit in air-conditioned comfort.

For mass passenger movement on land, the mode of tomorrow may well be tube vehicles. Such vehicles, operating in vacuum tubes at speeds as high as 500 m.p.h., are in the planning stage at the Federal test center for high speed ground transportation at Pueblo, Colo. Very little is known about the aerodynamics of flying a vehicle through a tube, so experimentation at Pueblo is starting with small-scale models.

Testing of improved water vehicles also is going on. The hydrofoils—jet-propelled ships on stilts—are operating in still, protected waters, but run into difficulties on the open sea. Engineers hope to make the vehicle practical enough for trans-oceanic travel.

Experimentation continues, too, on the so-called "hovercraft," which, by air pressure shot downward, can move along at high speeds above ground and water.

Pipelines—which can be overlooked, they are so unobtrusive—also are caught up in the technological revolution. Once used for carrying only water, oil and gas, they are now transporting in slurry form such normally solid materials as coal and iron ore. Engineers are working on the transportation of containers (capsules, canisters, plastic bags, etc.) that could be carried through pipes.

New concepts in aviation are just over the horizon. Pan American World Airways has plans in the making for a STOL (short takeoff and landing) system throughout the Northeast Corridor. STOL aircraft can land and take off on very short runways that can be laid down easily in downtown or close-to-town areas. Pan American's plan, known as Metroflight, calls for 16 such landing sites in various cities between Boston and Washington. "Metroflight can provide direct access to city centers, outlying trunk airports, suburbs and industrial areas," Pan Am says.

VTOL craft (vertical takeoff and landing) that can move up and down like helicopters and forward with the speed of regular planes are in the early stages of development.

For longer distances—and looking a bit beyond the horizon—there are those who envision rocket planes capable of flying from continent to continent at 17,000 m.p.h., a speed already exceeded by our spacecraft. One such plane already has been designed by engineers at a leading aircraft manufacturing corporation.

A steerable vehicle that can move around in space and return to earth intact is definitely in the future, and it's not too far out to suppose our grandchildren will be "honeymooning" on the moon. If they want to stay on earth, perhaps they would care for a weekend on the beach. What beach? Well, the Riviera may be quite popular with the Kansas City crowd for weekend jaunts in those days to come. Even for just a night on the town, Paris, London and Rome will be only moments away.

A Word About Containers

Containerization is expected to play a continually growing role in the transportation of goods across national and continental boundaries. As Eugene R. Birchler, Executive Vice President of Container Transport International, says, "Containers, more than any single innovation since steam powered ships, have caused a significant acceleration in international trade."

Utilizing computer controls and the stack concept used by multi-story parking garages, the new Containerport Development Corp. of New Jersey is building multi-story, vertical storage and retrieval systems for containers. They will be ten storage levels high and served by moving towers carrying vertical container hoists. "In general," says a spokesman for the corporation, "one moving tower and hoist would serve 500 container stalls, with each stall capable of storing one 40-foot container or two 20-foot containers. Each tower-mounted hoist is capable of lifting a container off a truck or railroad car, storing it, retrieving another container, and loading it onto a truck or railroad car within an average time of three minutes."

Much work is being done on the standardization of containers, which are becoming so important they may exert a major influence on product design. "It is already happening," says Vincent Grey, Engineering Manager for the Truck Trailer Manufacturers Association. "Designers always give priority to the ultimate usage . . . does it meet the need? Now they must be concerned with transportation cost. Many commodities are now being designed to permit transport by container. For example, a well-known American luxury automobile was designed so that four would fit into a container without damaging the finish."

Grey foresees the use of containers as storage and manufacturing units. "Like in the making of beer," he says. "Trucks would bring in the hops and malt in containers. These would be hooked up to a pipeline process that would carry the hops and malt, in proper quantities, to the mixing vats. When one container is emptied, you tap in a new one."

The military discovered that weather-proof containers make ideal rooms and adapting that concept and using the giant cargo-carrying helicopters, they have been airlifting completely furnished offices, field hospitals and barracks from one point to another in Vietnam.

Helicopters will be used more in the future in this country, particularly for special jobs around docks and to ferry in supplies to inaccessible places. They could even be used to ferry containers or possibly LASH (Lighter aboard ship handling) barges from manufacturer or warehouse or port to ships at sea. LASH takes containerization one step farther. Large floating barges, about 60 feet long and 30 feet wide, laden with standard-size containers, are actually towed out to the ship for loading and from the ship to port for unloading. They can get the mother ship in and out of ports in a matter of hours rather than days.

Where Man Will Live

"A megastructure would be something like 40 stories high and a mile in length. Any structure that large must have a large and complicated street network to service it. There would be separate functions. The top 50 percent might be residential, the next 20 percent offices and the lowest 30 percent would be for shopping, warehousing, distribution and maybe some kind of industry."

The speaker is Allen Dresdner, Chief of General Planning for Candeub, Fleissig and Associates of Newark, N.J., an urban planning consultant organization.

"You might well need a central receiving and distribution area where the trucks come in, unload and go out. The trucks might distribute over the entire megastructure, but then they might have the trucks, or even containers, hook up on fixed track and move around electrically."

This will be the metropolitan structure of the future, Dresdner believes, with residential, industrial, business, shopping, warehousing and distribution all operating together, like a small city in a big building. Schools, churches and recreation areas also would be included. One plan calls for such a megastructure to rise up a mountain in Southern California.

Architect Paolo Soleri foresees even larger megastructures, dwarfing today's largest skyscrapers and housing as many as 2.4 million residents, while in a recent television special, Actor-Narrator Lee Marvin talked about such exotic concepts as floating cities of 50,000 or more persons, which would actually be able to move about the world—going South for the winter, so to speak.

Transportation around the cities of the future might include a "dial-a-bus" system, as suggested by Don Fabun of Kaiser Aluminum & Chemical Corp. in his book, "The Dynamics of Change." One would dial a certain number, according to this concept, and when sufficient passengers were lined up, the bus—a small vehicle routed by computer—would pick up each passenger at his door. Starry-eyed as this may seem, the Department of Transportation already has conducted a series of experiments with this concept in Flint, Mich., and plans more experimentation in Haddonfield, N.J.

For downtown business and shopping areas, urban planner Dresdner sees little electric cars, like golf carts. "You would just drive 'em up the street and leave them for someone else to pick up," he says. "And when they needed to be regenerated, you would plug them into a socket."

Along these lines, Goodyear Tire & Rubber Co. has developed an in-town transportation system called "Carveyor System." Riders would board small wheel-less cars that ride on conveyor belts. They look like the vehicles used on roller-coasters and other amusement park rides. Boarding would take place from platforms that would be in constant motion at $1\frac{1}{2}$ m.p.h., the same speed as the cars. As the cars moved away from the station, they would pick up speed to as high as 15 m.p.h., and then they would slow down at the next station. San Jose plans to install a six-mile Carveyor system beginning in 1972.

Scientists at Johns Hopkins University's Applied Physics Laboratory in Silver Spring, Md., are pursuing the practicability of a car that would be powered by a flywheel. The flywheel would get its power from electricity, by being plugged in when not in use. When in use, the fast-spinning flywheel would generate electricity to run the car. (A more simplified version of flywheel energy is the toy car that is "wound up" by pumping its wheels against the floor before releasing the car to swish around the room.)

The Swiss have used the concept to make buses that reportedly ran regular routes in some Swiss and African cities.

"In fact there seems to be only one over-riding problem," the Wall Street Journal recently reported in a story on the flywheel car, "the automobile makers think the whole idea is nuts."

Perhaps so, but the government thinks enough of the idea that it has awarded the Johns Hopkins scientists a $190,000 contract to prove it one way or another.

Most automotive engineers agree with the automobile makers. Moreover, they are most interested in more practical, near-at-hand concepts, such as the traditional highly publicized turbine engine, the innovative Lear version, and the Wankel engine, with its triangular cylinders, lower weight-to-power ratio and fewer moving parts.

Some who foresee ever-increasing populations gathering in close quarters also see the sharing of buildings and facilities. Fabun suggests that man no longer needs to sleep at night, that this is a hangover from old, rural days when darkness by necessity spelled the end of the working day. Fabun says that man could work around the clock, sharing whole buildings and facilities, which now lay idle two-thirds of the time. One building could house an advertising firm during the day; a bank could take over from 4 p.m. to midnight, and an import-export business could use the facilities from midnight to 8 a.m., according to this concept.

Other facilities, such as manufacturing plants, also could be shared, like some competing newspapers today are sharing type-setting and press facilities.

Of course, all of these thoughts on megalopolitan living—or most of them, at least—tend to ignore the new mobility given to man by his motor vehicles. While city planners dream of megastructures, others see populations receding from the megalopolis, arguing that man moved to the city in search of work, but after finding it, he moved his residence back out to the country (Suburbia). Now that Suburbia has become densely populated, there may be movements farther out.

Man no longer needs to be near fixed lines of transportation, thanks to the motor car and truck and highway, and so the cities of the future may well be smaller—not larger—than today's metropolitan areas—and scattered.

In either case — megastructure or small, buckshot-patterned towns — the motor truck is going to have to assume an ever-increasing transportation burden.

Of Matter and Energy

We seldom stop to think about it, but there is as much iron and steel, aluminum, copper, zinc and other metals on this earth as there ever was. Unlike fuels, these are not "burned up"—they will be with us forever. The trouble is, economics governs the recycling of these materials, though steel in certain instances and such precious metals as gold and platinum are used over and over. Still, the day may not be too far off when man will know how to recycle all his metals economically, in which case the city dumps of today will be upgraded to the status of valuable mineral deposits.

Meanwhile, there still is a lot of ore under the ground and another vast source, virtually untouched, under the sea. Iron ore and sand from Tokyo Bay, tin ore from the ocean shelves and river beds of Malaya, Indonesia and Thailand, gold from Norton Sound in Alaska, and sulphur from the Gulf of Mexico—all attest to the rich mineral lodes under the sea.

There also is a vast store of potential food under the sea, scientists say, and underwater farming is a concept that has held the fancy of man for a number of years.

Still, man has not conquered the fathoms. He seems to have progressed further in adapting to the hostile environment of outer space.

However, much experimentation is going on beneath the sea. One device that holds great promise is an "artificial gill," a synthetic membrane of silicone rubber, which enables creatures to breathe while under water. The material has been used successfully as the walls of a cage holding submerged rabbits. In due time, man may be able to walk around the ocean floors wearing suits made of the material and be freed of the cumbersome underwater equipment in use today.

National Geographic Magazine suggests that the first real explorers of the ocean bottoms may be robots, "their microphone ears hearing things in frequencies humans cannot hear, their television eyes seeing things in the infrared portion of the spectrum."

As for energy, apprehension has been expressed by some that man will run out of energy sources. It is true that the better we live, the more energy we burn.

Transportation
and the
Technological
Revolution

A study by the Chase Manhattan Bank of New York reported that the per-capita use of energy in the United States has risen from 39 barrels of petroleum a year in 1950 to 49 barrels in 1965.

Sources of energy available to man include petroleum, natural gas, coal, waterpower, and nuclear fission. An article in a recent issue of The Sohioan, published by the Standard Oil Co. of Ohio, predicts more efficient recovering of oil and gas left in the ground after conventional methods have "played out" the well, economical extraction of oil from the nation's vast deposits of shale, and the conversion of coal to liquid fuels and pipeline-quality gas.

Buried in the earth, too, is a tremendous source of power that so far has been available only in those spots where it is near the surface. Just below the surface of the United States—as was pointed out in the first chapter—is enough heat stored to a depth of six miles to replace 900 trillion tons of coal! Where this geothermal power has been made available, it has proved itself. In Iceland, for example, steam from these hot spots has been used to heat homes since 1925.

"We used to think a geothermal field would last only forty years at most before becoming exhausted," says a United Nations official. "We are now beginning to think that a geothermal field, properly managed, may last forever."

John Lear, writing in a recent issue of Saturday Review, described his first view of geothermal power in action near Cerro Prieto, Mexico:

"I could see the pillar of water boiling into the sky, while our party was still miles away from the spout in the earth from which it spurted. I could hear the pillar's awesome roaring long before I came to stand beside it and learn that it was moving at the speed of sound. I felt no trace of dampness in the dry desert air as I stood there. Though only 20 percent of the pillar was steam, all but the steam evaporated within 100 feet of the ground—so enormous were the heat and pressure driving the water below."

Most exotic of all energy concepts and one that has excited scientists in countries all over the globe is that of nuclear fusion. The first atomic bomb was a fission bomb, made by splitting atoms, and nuclear power plants today are fission plants. But the hydrogen bomb was a fusion bomb—made by fusing atoms together. This is what is exciting the scientists: A successfully controlled fusion would give man unlimited energy at a very low cost. The key word is "controlled." So far, the scientists have not come up with a container capable of holding the tremendous heat necessary for fusion—more than 50 million degrees.

But they are on the way. The Washington Post, in an editorial for March 11, 1971, says an operating fusion reactor may be only 25 to 30 years away.

Such a reactor would not use scarce uranium, but deuterium, or heavy hydrogen, which is as handy as the nearest bucket of sea water.

"A successful fusion reactor would solve the energy problem for as long as we can see ahead," The Post editorial said. "It would be fueled by heavy hydrogen obtained from sea water. It would produce only energy and heat—no smoke, no dust, no radioactivity. Its output, in terms of energy, would be more electricity than most people have ever dreamed about at a cost far below that at which electricity is produced today. Two plants, if electricity could be moved and stored more efficiently than it is now, could, in theory, produce all the power the United States now uses. One plant could provide all the energy requirements most under-developed countries need to modernize. Sea water could be made usable at low cost, deserts could be made to bloom, the torpor of the tropic climate could be eliminated through air conditioning, the frigid areas at the Poles could be opened up, and so on."

Conclusion

There is a natural inclination to equate the world of tomorrow with science fiction. It is thus safely removed from reality, until tomorrow becomes today—which it always does, inevitably—and then man is there, actually living in what was yesterday's fantasy.

Still, man has adjusted. The idea of flying from New York to San Francisco in less than five hours was a fantastic unreality a generation ago. Today it is commonplace. The idea of television in everyone's living room was the subject of "way-out" discussions a few years ago. Today television is in everyone's living room. Moreover, it turns a number of people off, who seldom turn theirs on. So quickly does the novelty of man's ingenious products wear off, that the magic of transporting pictures and sound, live, from 240,000 miles in space has actually begun to bore great numbers of people. (Remember when man listened to the radio? Today men wonder exactly what they did do with their eyes while listening to Pepper Young and One Man's Family on radio.)

Today's changes are coming with unprecedented swiftness, as some social scholars have pointed out—in some cases with apprehension. We believe that the apprehension is unfounded. Little boys and girls have always recovered from Christmas and man has always adjusted to the new settings in man's continuously improving drama. The adjustments we refer to are adjustments to changes for the better. What indeed would be difficult—in fact, disastrous—would be the need to adjust to a worsening existence, the supreme folly of going back in time, all the way back to before the Stone Age, as Konrad Lorenz has warned.

And these are really the only alternatives: To keep going forward, or to retreat to the primitive state. There is no middle ground, no stopping man's fantastic voyage in mid-course and holding the position—though there are some who preach such an indefensible line of inaction.

In this chapter, we have examined some of the areas of recent technological advancement, though admittedly not in depth. We have looked at the earthbound marvels produced by the space program and noted the tremendous changes being fashioned by that spectacular electronic brain, the computer. We touched on some of the changes the computer is fashioning in transportation and speculated on improvements among the various modes in the future. We noted the possible changes in man's cities and new sources of metals and power.

So vast is the overall subject that we could have covered only one aspect of it in a manuscript many times the size of this study. And we could have gone off into different areas than the ones covered.

But in the final analysis, the essentials would have been the same: Man is living in a fast-changing world. Tremendous breakthroughs in electronics, space exploration, computers and other areas are raising man faster and faster, farther and farther from a life of drudgery and discomfiture that was the common lot of most men just a few years ago.

Given the freedom and encouragement to expand, this union between science and technology will produce more goods for more people than is dreamed of today. When you come down to it, that is what it is all about anyway: More of the good life for more people.

But that's what it *always* has been about.

For the technological revolution is not new. It began when some creature in the dark, dismal past picked up a stick or a branch and made the awesome discovery that he had the capability of using nature's products to make his own life better. It has been going on ever since. Major early breakthroughs included fire and the wheel. Others included the lever and the pulley and the domestication of beasts. And while there were times when technology seemed at a standstill, it never has been thoroughly extinguished, for man has always sought better ways of doing thing, always, of course, motivated by the search for the better life.

And so the technological advancement continued, as man found better ways to erect buildings, bring water to his fields and homes, to transport his goods and himself. Along came steam—and they called that the Industrial Revolution. Electricity, internal combustion engines, automobiles and trucks, and airplanes followed, and on their heels have come jet airplanes, space craft, computers, electronics—and they call this the Technological Revolution, to distinguish it from what went before, to make it more understandable.

What has all this to do with transportation and marketing? Everything. For transportation and marketing make up the team that carries the ball—and everything else, for that matter. What good would it do to produce enough bread for every table, if there were no way to get the bread from the bakery to the tables? What good would it do to know how to send man to the moon—a transportation advancement in itself—if there were no way to transport the essential products to the launching site?

Without transportation there would be no technological revolution. And without technology, transportation and marketing wouldn't have a wheel to ride on.

Transportation and marketing have never operated in a vacuum. They must keep pace with the world around them. To do less would mean failure and would cause that world to come crashing down.

We cannot stand still! We must see to it that all transportation and marketing keep pace. We must see to it that our airlines exploit all available technologies in the never-faltering goal of perfect efficiency. The same is true of our railroads, our trucking industry, our ships at sea and on our inland waterways, and our pipe lines.

For transportation is not only important to man's progress; it is vital to man's progress!

When the first primeval creature picked up the first stick—perhaps to help ward off an enemy—he was accepting a challenge, not from the enemy, but from an ally—Nature. "Discover me, use me," Nature challenged. Man has been meeting that challenge ever since, until now, today, man's response to the challenge—technology—has become a challenge in itself. There are those who say man's

Transportation
and the
Technological
Revolution

technology is ruining man by despoiling his environment. There are others who say that man is too weak mentally to cope with the marvels of his technology. Still others sing the suicidal dirge of retreat, chanting that technology is an evil in itself.

But the anti-technologists might as well also tell us that the sun should be turned off on the grounds that it causes sunburn, melts mountain snows that cause floods, and starts forest fires.

We believe the great technological revolution is a promise, not a problem. But it is also a challenge—a challenge that should be most welcome because the road to a better life has been paved with challenges. And no one has a greater challenge in this fast-changing world of miracles than you who are in the transportation and marketing field.

If those in transportation and marketing try to operate in 1980 and beyond with 1970's technology and equipment and have not geared themselves to carry significantly more goods to a geographically dispersing—as well as a numerically expanding—population, then the Golden Age may well turn out to be made of Fool's Gold.

But transportation and marketing have always met their challenges. That is why they were able to carry man truly to the gates of the Golden Age. And that is why they will carry man through those gates to a new way of life, where science and technology and man's dedication to serving man will combine to create an era of splendor that would surpass today's most ambitious fantasies. Let us not tarry.

"Of all inventions, the alphabet and
the printing press alone excepted,
those inventions which abridge distance
have done most for the civilization
of our species."

—Thomas Babington Macaulay

79

published by
Public Relations Department
American Trucking Associations
Washington, D.C.
January, 1972

Sponsored by UNITED STATES STEEL

as a project of the ATA Foundation